Wallace Nutting

FURNITURE
OF THE PILGRIM CENTURY

(OF AMERICAN ORIGIN)   1620-1720

with maple and pine to 1800,
including colonial utensils and
wrought-iron house hardware
into the 19th century

Illustrated with more than 1500 examples

COMPLETELY REVISED AND GREATLY ENLARGED

In two volumes   Volume Two

DOVER PUBLICATIONS, INC., NEW YORK

CONTENTS

The references are to text pages only

Volume Two

This Dover edition, first published in 1965, is an unabridged and unaltered republication of the revised and enlarged edition published by the Old American Company in 1924.

For this Dover edition the work has been divided into two volumes. Volume One contains pages 1 through 398 and Volume Two contains pages 399 through 714. For convenience of reference, Figures 532 through 571, which occupy pages 403-6, 409-12 and 415-17, and thus fall in Volume Two, are also reproduced at the end of Volume One, since the text references to these figures occur in Volume One.

International Standard Book Number: 0-486-21471-0
Library of Congress Catalog Card Number: 65-26030

Manufactured in the United States of America

Dover Publications, Inc.
180 Varick Street
New York, N. Y. 10014

DAY BEDS, SETTEES AND SETTLES

THE day bed, which is commonly called a couch in England, and a chaise longue in France, is most aptly described by the last name since it is really a chair with a seat drawn out to the length of a bed. The back is precisely like that of a chair in most instances. The first set of feet under the back are often in a square section like that of a chair back of the period. Thus the true day bed never has its ends alike. A loose commercial term for a single bed with a head and foot is day bed. Doubtless it came in through a desire to render such single beds popular, or perhaps through ignorance. Ancient day beds with two ends were non-existent so far as we know. In England there was a sofa or upholstered settee, as we may name it, in the seventeenth century but it was extremely rare. The only example we have seen in this country is in the Essex Institute, and we do not know that an American origin is claimed for it. We have seen a double ended settee of the Sheraton period. We confine ourselves here, therefore, to the day bed, as it is the only type known in America during its period.

The genesis of the day bed is unknown, like the beginnings of most other things in this world. We have sometimes found a duchesse of a later period, which is built like a short day bed, with a stool which can be moved up at the foot, and built to match it, so as to secure the length of a couch. The charm of a day bed consists in its lines, as they relate themselves to chairs of the period. Such interest has been excited in late years that these articles are practically all gathered in by collectors as rapidly as they are found. Perhaps a score or two are known in addition to the Pennsylvania day bed of which there may be as many more.

It will be observed that they never have a back. The head is the back.

No. 572. A day bed belonging to the Metropolitan Museum. The stretchers are carved and pierced and arched in a manner practically the same as that of chairs in the Flemish style, dating from 1680 to 1700.

A feature of the construction is that we do not find a scrolled stretcher at the foot. The piece was intended, of course, to be placed at the side of a room. The foot stretcher is set low to correspond with the cross stretchers, between the others pairs of legs. As a rule these pieces are made on both sides alike. That is, they had no backs except the head, and were symmetrical and appropriate wherever placed. In the more elegant pieces as here the back and the seat are caned. In this example the legs are turned, though the principal stretchers and the back or head are carved.

Another feature of these day beds is that the head is usually hinged, swinging down at the top on dowel pins which run from the frame of the head into the posts near the main frame of the day bed. These features are occasionally absent, and where they were originally present we sometimes find that the swinging head has been fastened in an immovable position like a chair back. The swing of the head was regulated by a chain which passed through the posts or was attached to them so that the head might be thrown down into a horizontal position or given any angle for comfort. Possibly this arrangement was made in deference to the occasional use of the day bed as a bed. The frame is usually a little short for a bed, and the letting down of the head serves to lengthen the frame. The specimen before us belongs to the walnut period.

No. 573. This simple day bed shows the method of lacing or trussing the canvas where such a basis was used for a cushion. We may presume that the cane seats were often provided with cushions. At least they would otherwise have gone to pieces quickly. The arrangement to receive the cushion here is similar to that in many old fashioned beds, using a canvas instead of a rope support.

Owner: The Metropolitan Museum.

Nos. 574–576. A room in the Captain Brown House, the house of the Antiquarian Society in Concord. The remarkably handsome day bed shown in the corner of this room belonged to the Rev. Peter Bulkeley, the first minister of Concord, and the chair which is seen to match it was his chair of dignity, appertaining to his office. These pieces, having been designed to go together, are among our richest treasures of that period. In fact, the collection of this society, though smaller than the collections of the great cities, consists of a good number of very choice specimens, so much so that it is perhaps not rivaled in New England by any other public collection.

No. 577. A simpler day bed belonging to the George F. Ives Collection. It will be noted that this is all turned and that even the post at the back is as near like the other posts as it may be and still afford a space for the mortise of the main rail. Upholstery on these day beds is very rare and probably always out of place. We do not believe that in this case the upholstery should be attached. It will be noted here that the head is rather plain and composed of three splats, if we may use that term of wide banisters.

Specimens like this or indeed any of the day beds are very light and easily movable, by which we infer that it was the intention to place them temporarily where they were most convenient.

No. 578.   A turned day bed, the property of Mr. Edward C. Wheeler, Jr. This bed shows a proper cushion added to a foundation such as that of No. 573. The true stretchers at the head are a very unusual feature. One also sees here that the rails are mortised into the post at the foot, and do not run over the foot posts as in the other examples so far shown. This assimilates the day bed more closely to the chair. The bulb and ring turning is the usual style of the end of the seventeenth and the beginning of the eighteenth century, unless we have carving.

No. 579.   This day bed gives a good example of the development from a chair. Thus it will be seen that the back or head has legs precisely like a chair of the period, and that the front end or foot has Spanish feet, like the front legs of a chair. The intermediate sets of legs are plainly turned. The head in this case is the true Dutch fiddle back, Dutch in this connection referring to the types brought in under William and Mary and Queen Anne.

The upholstery here has now been removed and a leather cushion put in its place. The canvas bottom is found. The day bed is of walnut. There was an inscription attached to the underside stating that the piece belonged to Clarissa Griswold of Killingworth, Connecticut, from which state the piece came. This piece is longer than usual, being 74 inches over all. The width is $21\frac{3}{4}$ inches. The hight of the head is $37\frac{1}{4}$ inches. The frame is 14 inches high.

No. 580. ˙ A prettily turned day bed with a paneled head. This panel being solid differentiates it from other examples. Here also is first seen plainly the arrangement for swinging the head.

All the specimens we have so far shown have eight legs, a style more sought for and regarded better than the six legged type.

Owner: Mr. L. G. Myers.

No. 581.   A heavily turned day bed. We have here the Dutch splat in the back, which in this case seems designed originally to be fixed.

It will be seen that in the framing of a piece like this it is important that the cross members should enter the posts at a different level from the lengthwise stretchers. Thus there is ample room for mortises without weakening the legs. As an example of turning, this is an attractive day bed. The maker was called upon, owing to his chosen method of construction, to devise a very long turning for the side stretchers, which he has successfully accomplished.

Size: 72 inches long, $26\frac{3}{4}$ inches wide, $16\frac{3}{4}$ inches high on the frame. The head is $36\frac{3}{4}$ inches high.

Owner: The estate of William G. Erving, M.D., of Washington.

No. 582. A Spanish foot day bed with an extraordinary number of stretchers. We have never elsewhere seen anything like the two additional longitudinal sets which are mortised into the cross members below. The effect is not unpleasing. A much greater degree of strength was secured. In this specimen we have for the first time all of the feet carved in the Spanish fashion, and very well done. Of course, the original thought of the chaise longue was departed from in carving the feet at the back or head.

The head here is elaborate and handsome. The wood is walnut, as in most cases of elegant construction. We are more apt to find maple in the simpler specimens.

Owner: Mr. Martin Gay of Hingham.

No. 583. A Pennsylvania day bed. These specimens are interesting for themselves and also because they undoubtedly foreshadow, and at no distant period, the beginning of Windsor construction. In fact, the "blunt arrow" type of construction found on the feet, and the general turning of the leg, is precisely like that found in the earliest specimens of Windsor arm chairs, though of course the posts here are larger. There is the curious effect in this specimen of slanted back posts, which omit the usual angle at the frame. That angle required a rather special adeptness with a lathe.

The head is of reeded banisters running above into an arched and molded rail. The average size of the turning of the legs in Pennsylvania beds is about two and a half inches. The same heavy bulb and ring stretcher is used as appears in the Queen Anne furniture. The top rail of the back was made long enough to strike against the posts when the head was drawn up, and thus to prevent the head falling forward on the seat.

In some specimens the central pair of side stretchers on the Pennsylvania beds is set at a different hight from the side pairs, in order not to weaken the wood. From a structural standpoint this scheme is good, but to borrow an expression from automobiles, it loses the stream line effect.

In all the examples we have seen of the Pennsylvania day bed the seats were covered with rush. The pieces are very comfortable, substantial and quaint articles of furniture.

Owner: Mr. Hollis French.

No. 584. A specimen of the Pennsylvania day bed, in which the reeded banisters of the back enter a semi-circular crested top rail, which is heavily molded to correspond with the outline of the arch.

532. TURNED DUTCH CHAIR. 1720–30.

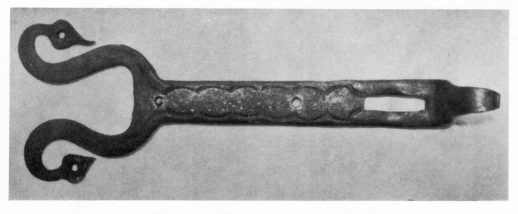

533. A PENNSYLVANIA ETCHED HASP. LATE 18th CENTURY.

534–535. A Dutch and a Serpentine Child's Chair. 1710–20.

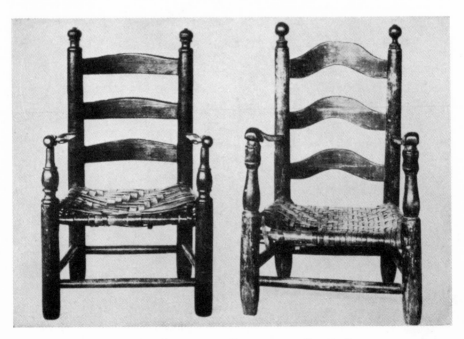

536–537. New England and Pennsylvania Child's Chairs.

538. Arched Banister Back.

539. Comb Corner Chair.

540. Child's Wing Chair.

541. VERY EARLY JOINT STOOL. 1640–60.

542. CHILD'S CHAIR.

543. BANISTER BACK.

In neither of these Pennsylvania day beds that we show does the ball at the foot of the post exhibit the best characteristic mark. In a specimen of the author's collection which is not shown, this ball is very markedly larger in diameter than any other part of the post, and the appearance is distinctive.

We see here that the back posts, while turned above, are of a square section below, after the analogy of the chair. As a kind of concession, however, to the rest of the construction the square legs are roughly notched near the bottom.

This piece was in the former collection of the author.

The owner is not known to the author.

No. 585. A day bed in the estate of J. Milton Cobourn, M.D. This singular and interesting piece is evidently a country made specimen. The stretchers instead of being turned or carved are cut like the skirt of a table, and are run around the entire frame at the same level. The head also is not made to swing but the top rail is imposed upon the posts, and a large number of banisters or spindles are inserted. Nevertheless, the legs have turned sections, as well as the upper parts of the head. We may presume that the maker was removed from the direct influence of an established style, and therefore worked from memory or from his own ideas.

We may remark as we close the subject of day beds that their existence indicates that our ancestors had not the iron constitutions with which they have been credited. The day bed indicates that they sometimes found it agreeable, and did not consider it immoral, to enjoy a siesta. We might, it is true, point out that the shortness of the couch portion may indicate that these pieces were used for resting in the bed chambers, and by the ladies only. We do not know that there is any ancient evidence as to the rooms in which these pieces were usually placed.

No. 586. A day bed in the full Flemish design. This beautiful piece in walnut carries out completely the Flemish scroll in the design of the leg, and the stretchers It will be noticed that the arch of the carved stretcher in this case is filled with a pair of scrolls and is pierced. Undoubtedly this method of construction was in the interest of strength and we believe it is sometimes found in chairs. This elegant piece has often been seen at the annual exhibit of the Arts and Crafts Society at Hingham. It is in good condition, and the existence of the balls or shoes on the feet indicate that it has always had good care. The head of this piece does not show very well but it is excellently carved.

Owner: Mrs. Rogers of Hingham.

No. 587–588. No. 587 is a child's settle. We see here the analogy of the pine chest, in that the settle has no frame, but that the front board is nailed directly to the scrolled end.

The finger holes at the back corresponding with that of the wing chair on the right are interesting. Although these pieces are now found together we cannot suppose that they were made to go together, otherwise the scroll of the wing would match in both specimens. The boring of the holes rather than cutting out a larger piece is in the interest of retaining the strength of the wood, for the material here is pine.

Although we have called the larger piece a child's settle it is entirely possible from its size that it was a pung seat. Indeed the author owned such a seat in precisely the same construction, which showed on the outside of the ends the wearing away of the red paint where the end had come in contact with the side board of the pung.

The settle in its pine board form was the furniture of persons in moderate circumstances or, since it was placed as a rule in the kitchen, it was made thus simple for every day use.

We have not seen an American carved settee or settle, though we have seen such a settee on which new carving had been done to pass it off as an unique American piece.

No. 589. A small scrolled settle. The shape of the scrolls on the end boards of this settle suggest somewhat the crude carving in imitation of the limbs of an evergreen. The shortness of the piece adds to its interest.

Owner: Mrs. De Witt Howe of Manchester, New Hampshire.

The material is pine.

No. 590. A miner's candle stick. The flat scroll which receives the candle is made as a spring to grasp closely. The candle stick could either be thrust into the wall of the mine or hung up. Very elaborate specimens of these miner's candles are known in Pennsylvania, one of them being a work of art.

No. 591–592. A settle bed. At this writing this piece is the only one known of its kind in America. The author owned this for some time before he knew what it was. Below in No. 593 it is shown as used in the day time. An Irishman who happened one day to see it exclaimed, " Well, if there ain't a settle bed! I was raised in one of them things." It is said that they are found in Ireland in oak, and there is a report that they are known in Poland.

This piece is in hard and soft pine. The eleven deep panels of the back are framed and pinned so far as their rails and stiles are concerned. One board, however, covers the length of all and is of course not a true

544.　Spanish-Dutch Chair.　　　　545.　Early Dutch Chair.

546–547.　Pennsylvania Lamps.

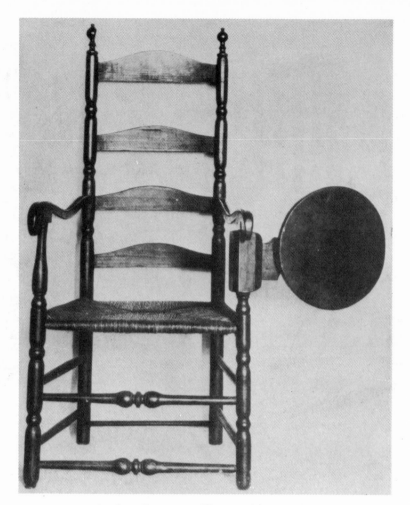

548. Slat Back with Writing Arm. 1720–30.

549. Turned Joint Stool.

550–551. Pair of Unique Chair Stools 1690–1710.

552. A Long Turned Joint Stool. 1680–1700.

553. Splayed Joint Stool.

554. Heavy Joint Stool.

555. Light Joint Stool.

panel. The panels in front are true. The seat swings out and down and is boxed at the ends, and was never built into the frame of the settle. It was attached by hooks and staples, a portion of which still remain in place. A feather bed was used, so that the bed and the covering would easily shut up into the confined space. The ends have panels like those on the front. The arms are of the wainscot chair type but are of pine. The front edges of the frame at the ends under the arms are very strongly molded.

Size: Length outside 74 inches. The back is 36¾ inches high. The seat is 14 inches wide and 17¾ inches high. The frame at the ends and the arms are 1⅝ inches thick.

Origin: Found on the North Shore of Massachusetts in 1922.

We have here, therefore, a framed settle or more properly settee, a term which is restricted to framed seats.

The quilt is of a quaint pattern.

No. 594. A framed settee. The wood is maple, as to the turned parts. The seat and panels and frame in the back are of yellow pine. The back sill is of oak. This piece was found in Connecticut in 1922. So far as it has come to our observation it is the only framed settee analogous to the English type. It supplies the long desired missing link, to go with our rare American wainscot chairs with the scrolled arm.

Size: Length over all, 75 inches; width over all 27 inches, which includes the rolled end of the arms. Hight over all including extension of back posts, 50½ inches. Width of seat 20½ inches; hight of seat, 18¼ inches. The square of the turned posts is 2¼ inches. The back posts are 1¼ inches by 2½ inches. The arms are 1½ inches thick.

No. 595. A New York wagon seat. We give these seats the name because most of them seem to be derived from New York state, though they have been found in western Connecticut and Massachusetts and probably in northern Pennsylvania and New Jersey. They were used alternately as seats in market wagons, held in place by the side boards, and as small love seats in the dwellings. A characteristic is the middle post, which is made larger than the end posts.

This specimen is from the collection of Mr. Chauncey C. Nash.

Size: 29 inches high. The seat is 13 inches high, wagon seats always being lower than chair seats. The surface of the seat is 14 by 33½ inches. A great many of these specimens have been brought into the market within recent years. The seats are mostly in rush, but we find an occasional one in splint.

No. 596. An amusing spring wagon seat.

Owner: Collection of George F. Ives.

The construction is sufficiently obvious to need no explanation, but we may say that ordinary wagon seats were often built with the same spring construction. The turnings here are very much better than we ordinarily see.

No. 597. A quaint small rocker settle. The foot rest is concaved. Doubtless the intention was to raise the feet from the floor for the sake of warmth. The settle seems to have been "built for two." The immediate derivation is from New York, but we presume it is a Jersey or Pennsylvania piece.

Relating to the date it might be, judging from the habits of the people of the region, any time in the eighteenth century.

No. 598. New York wagon seat with spindles. In this specimen some effort has been made at ornamentation by setting a portion of the spindles on a diagonal. It will be noted that we have here an arm which runs over the top of the post and is connected with it by a dowel. On the other hand in No. 596 we have the earlier method of construction by which the dowel runs into the side of the post.

Owner: Mr. Rudolph P. Pauly.

No. 599. A cradle in oak, perhaps English. We show it here in order to give a progressive demonstration of the development of the cradle as it was found in America.

No. 600. A pine board settle with panels. A piece of this sort made with two rows of panels is now considerably sought for.

Owner: The Collection of George F. Ives.

One notices the method of setting the little candle sconce in the center. The settle ends here are very high.

Size: 64 inches long, the back is 52 inches high. The seat is 16 inches deep and the hight is the same. The arms are 35 inches high.

The advantage of paneling the backs of settles was slight, so far as use was concerned. Paneling was somewhat more finished but entirely unnecessary. Of course, when found paneled, as here, they are successors of the English tradition of oak paneling.

We do not seem to find cushions for settles, but no doubt they were sometimes used. The seats are never shaped, and therefore are rather uncomfortable. Usually the seat was hinged when the settle was boxed in below. In this case the base was used, sometimes for a wood box, as the piece was kept near the fire, or sometimes for a grain chest. Indeed, the development of the settle from the chest is obvious.

No. 601–602. This is the only example that we happen to have seen of a built in settle. It is in a seventeenth century house in Wrentham, and has a single end only. It is set back over the sill of the house and

556. Joint Stool with Drawer. 1680–1700.

557–566. Candles and Lamps.

567. WINDSOR HIGH CHAIR. 1720.

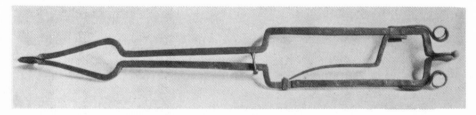

568. UNUSUAL PIPE TONGS. 18th CENTURY.

569. HIGH STRETCHER SQUAB. 1680–1700.

570–571. JOINT STOOLS. 1660–1700.

572. SCROLL STRETCHER DAY BED. 1680–1700.

573. ALL TURNED DAY BED. 1690–1700.

the sheathed paneling of the outside wall forms the back. It is quaint and small and most interesting. The door handles and latches here shown are original on the house and are of wood. We know no reason why we may not consider the settle as contemporaneous with the house.

No. 603. A large pine paneled settle, the property of the Rhode Island School of Design. The knob-like terminals of the scrolled end boards are interesting. Also one should notice that there is a board laid over the back at the top in the form of a hood. Of course the object was to keep off the wind, as these pieces were drawn up before the great fire-places. There was a frost line on the floor in bitter weather, as referred to in Whittier's " Snowbound." In these settles the back board behind the seat usually ran to the floor to stop the movement of cold air. In many cases the end board was not scrolled as here but was made solid for purposes of protection against cold.

If we consider the settle in its modern use we feel that it interferes with the unity of the house, as it cuts off the view of the fireplace. It shuts the fireplace away from the rest of the room. Therefore, in the arrangement of a settle in an old house it is better to place it on the side wall at right angles with the fireplace.

The Rhode Island School of Design possesses a second settle very similar to this.

Size: 74 inches long, 53½ inches high, and 20 inches deep.

CRADLES

W E DO not know when or where the cradle originated. We regret its discontinuance as an article of household furniture, because about it is enshrined so much of sentiment. After all is said and done, the sentiment in relation to antique furniture is, to us, at least, a great part of its charm. It is said that cradles are not good for the health of a child. Happily, we do not have to pass on that subject. The hand that rocked the cradle now places the child in a bed or crib, theoretically; but practically, most mothers put their children in baby carriages, to do duty instead of cradles.

There is an interesting question as to the origin of the rocking chair. An Englishman told the author that his mother had bounced back and forth with him in her arms, on a flat-bottomed chair, until she had worn the base into a roughly rounded form. This is a very amusing sidelight upon the lack of rockers in England. It raises the question whether or not rockers in this country may not have come in about the time that cradles began to go out. It may be that their original use was to carry out the idea that the English mother was working out so blindly. At any rate, the cradle was not rocked with the hand, as the politicians would tell us, but by the foot, so that the hands might be available for knitting or mending. In practice, of course, the cradle would be for the most part rocked by an older child.

We do not often find cribs in the earliest American period. In fact, no such article has come to our attention. We may safely assume that the cradle or the trundle bed served instead of cribs. The cradle was a necessity in the home room, or the fire room, because there was not room in it for a bed, and there was no heat in the bedroom. The child must be under the mother's eye and in a comfortable place. We have seen cradles which bore at the foot the mark of heat blisters from the effect of the fire.

The hearth really became the sacred spot in our ancestral history. The baby was born by the hearth, was rocked there, and later crept about it, and got his first lessons in chemistry and poetry by watching the blaze. At a later period, it was at the hearth that his education began, as he stood between, or sat upon, his grandfather's knees, and heard the tales of long ago. There, also, he conned his horn book, or read of Bunyan's Pilgrim, by the light of pine knots. At the hearth, as a youth,

574–576. Day Bed and Corresponding Chairs. 1680–1700.

577. Day Bed, Banister Head. 1690–1710.

578.   TURNED DAY BED.   1690–1710.

579.   TURNED AND SPANISH FOOT DAY BED.   1690–1710.

580. Unusually Turned Day Bed. 1690–1710.

581. A Six Legged Dutch Day Bed. 1700–1710.

582. DOUBLE STRETCHER DAY BED. 1690–1710.

583. PENNSYLVANIA DAY BED. 1710–30.

he held his sweetheart's hand.   Here he was married.   Here, surrounded by his children, he passed the evenings of his middle age.   Here, as an ancient, he sat in the chimney corner, in the cool days of the early fall and late spring, and warmed his hands at the small fire kept up for his comfort; and here he passed on to his fathers.

The cradle, the beginning of the seven ages of man, is, therefore, for us Americans, an object of no little interest.   Nevertheless, the mahogany or light maple cradle, which is found in almost every attic, is scorned by the collector, because it is not ancient nor rare enough to attract us, nor is it wanted about under foot.   A use, indeed, has been found for it of late.   We notice in a great many households where antique furniture is used, that the cradle has become the woodbox for the fireplace.

Of course, in this volume, we confine ourselves to the very early examples which are either so ancient or so good in themselves as to be highly regarded.

No. 604.   A walnut cradle, originating in Pennsylvania.   It has a scrolled head and foot board, with a heart-shaped hand hold for lifting about.   There is also a scrolled bracket at the head board.   The piece is framed, having large corner posts ending in rude balls.   One notices the knobs at the side, which were used to button down the coverlet.   In Pennsylvania, cradles were used to a date later, probably, than in New England.   We do not know, when we reach Pennsylvania, that someone may not be making furniture as his first great-grandsire did at the time of the settlement.   They love the old ways even more than the people of Connecticut.   It is safe, however, to place a cradle of this sort in the eighteenth century, with the caution that similar cradles may have been made much later.

It is apparent that the sides of this cradle are raked, that is, splayed. We shall see later that the very earliest cradles had vertical sides.

No. 605.   A cradle with a gallery and with spindles at the sides of the hood.

Owner: The Rhode Island School of Design.

This cradle is remarkable in having a fascinating low gallery around the sides and the foot.   It terminates near the hood against brackets. The balls of this cradle are in excellent condition.   It requires slight attention to see that cradles of this sort were made after the analogy of the chest.   It has its panels, its corner posts, and its channel molds on the rails and stiles.   This cradle probably had some sort of a cap to its hood. In the uncertainty as to its precise form, however, it is better to leave it as it is.   It is said to have been found near Abington, Massachusetts, about 1920.   Its sides are vertical.

No. 606. A flax breaker, such as was used in the seventeenth, eighteenth, and probably the beginning of the nineteenth century. The flax
was placed in the form in which it came from the field, under the huge
wooden maul, which by repeated blows disintegrated the stem into fibres,
until, through the use of the hatchel, it was at last reduced to a sufficiently
fine condition to be spun.

No. 607. The Dr. Samuel Fuller cradle. Although no lives have
yet been lost in battles around this cradle, it has excited so much interest
and controversy as to be a kind of monument among antiques. It was
through one of the Alden family that the author was referred to the
Cushman family, related to the Aldens, as the owners of this cradle. The
Cushmans inherited it through intermarriage with the Fullers. There is
an unbroken tradition that it came from Dr. Samuel Fuller of the Mayflower. So far, the tradition seems thoroughly credible, because the
manifest age of the piece should take it back to 1650 at least.

The tradition then goes on to say that Peregrine White was rocked in
this cradle on the Mayflower. As Peregrine is also said to have been
rocked in a wicker cradle now in Pilgrim Hall, Plymouth, and even is,
by some, said to have been rocked in the cradle in a glass case in that
hall, we must conclude, if any of these tales are true, that Peregrine was,
to use a Southern phrase, the rockingest child, as well as the first white
child born in New England. First he was rocked in the cradle of the
deep, and being born in Provincetown Harbor, was supposed to have been
rocked in the cradle here shown, since it was handily available in the
lading of the Mayflower, whereas the wicker cradle was hard to get at.
It was, of course, presumed that the arrival in America would long precede
the birth of the child.

An artist who has painted one of the large Pilgrim pictures at the
Hall has shown one of the Pilgrim fathers wrestling with a cradle as
he gets it aboard the Mayflower. We use the word " wrestle " advisedly,
because, as a friend of ours said, with a sardonic grin, the cradle is large
enough to rock a bull calf in. However that may be, the cradle is
purely American. Its side panels are all pine, though its end panels are
all American oak, and of course, also, the frame. The hood, however,
is of pine. It is notch carved on the ends, and molded on the front and
back, and a border is scratch carved in a diamond pattern. This is one of
the important features of the cradle, since so many ancient examples have
lost the cap board of the hood.

A second feature of great importance, and possibly marking unique-
ness in American cradles, is the carrying of the gallery around three sides
of the hood. The gallery at the back is composed of short spindles. The

584. PENNSYLVANIA DAY BED. 1710–30.

585. COUNTRY MADE DAY BED. 1710–40.

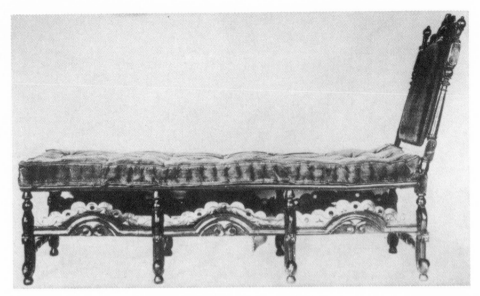

586. Flemish Couch. 1680–1700.

587–588. Child's Settle and Wing Chair. 1730–80.

589. Small Pine Settle, Scrolled End. 1730–80.

590. Miner's Light.

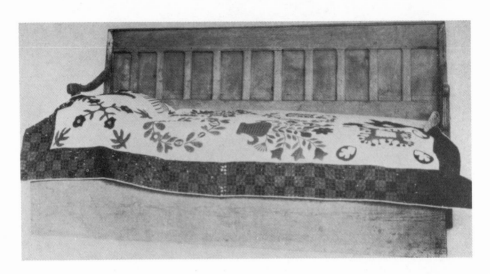

591–592. SETTLE BED MADE UP. 1710–40.

593. SETTLE BED CLOSED. 1710–40.

supposed purpose of the gallery was to allow the mother a peep at the child from whatever angle she viewed the cradle. The turnings of the spindles are practically identical with those found on the earlier Carver chairs.

A third item of great interest is the split spindle, not so rare on the inside of the gallery opening, attached to the frame; but unique, up to the time of the present writing, as attached in the form of a long, specially turned drop or split spindle on the front of the hood. The sides of the cradle are vertical, and it is very deep. The stiles and the rails are strongly cut in channel molds and double pinned. There is a chamfer around the panels. In fact, what we have here is really a chest in which a hood is substituted for a lid; that is to say, the chest construction is modified sufficiently to form a cradle. The projecting foot-posts are in the earliest form of turning. The cradle has never been painted. An interesting feature is observed here in relation to the quartering of the oak of the frame. Those portions which are featured show dark. In a piece that is finished by shellac or varnish, they show light, as compared with the rest of the wood.

Of course the cradle was made in America, and in Plymouth, but whether by John Alden or Kenelm Winslow, we, of course, do not know. An amusing fact in relation to this cradle is that there is now being sold in Plymouth, as has been the case for many years, a picture of the cradle as being the one now in Pilgrim Hall under the glass case. We are assured by a lady who was rocked in this cradle as an infant, as have been every one of her American ancestors, that she knows absolutely the whereabouts of the cradle during her life, and that it has never been in Pilgrim Hall. Certainly it is quite unlike the example now there, which is not a paneled cradle. On it thin strips of maple or beech are applied and nailed to form false panels on the pine boards beneath. One of these strips at the foot has become detached, and the observer can plainly see the discoloration of the wood where it once was. The old stories indicate how cursory and uncritical, and in many cases, really untruthful, matters connected with antique furniture can be.

The cradle in Pilgrim Hall has very pretty spindle work over the head, instead of a cap for the hood. In that particular it is important. It is also, doubtless, important for a historical reason in connection with another branch of the Fuller family.

Our Samuel Fuller cradle is a most satisfactory specimen, from the mellow and worn condition of the wood, and from its Pilgrim origin, and especially from its intrinsic merit.

A number of years since, the author replaced the missing rockers with oak cut from the f~ce of an exposed beam in the Marsh House, Wethersfield, the oldest house in town. This oak is of precisely the same color and consistency as the rest of the cradle, so that, unless one points out the inner surfaces of these rockers, it is hard to persuade even a critic that they are not original.

Size: The square of the posts is $2\frac{1}{2}$ inches. The cradle is $34\frac{1}{2}$ inches long, 33 inches high, and $19\frac{1}{2}$ inches wide. These dimensions do not include the side extensions of the rockers.

Nos. 608–611. A picture showing an early eighteenth century room. The bed is of the second period, when the hangings were still retained at the head, but were reduced at the sides and the foot merely to an upper and a lower valance.

The quaint little child's chair before the fireplace is worthy of attention. The chair nearest the bed has its back posts running up above the main frame of the back section, as is the fashion in Spanish chairs. Hence this chair is not otherwise shown. A quaint little looking glass on the wall has a leather frame.

No. 612. A cradle in maple, swinging on posts. This quaint and odd device is sometimes seen on later mahogany cradles, as in one beautiful specimen at the Essex Institute, Salem. In the cruder form here exhibited we have the shoe, or base, run crosswise at the ends below the posts, and a longitudinal stretcher on the floor. The cradle swings on heavy wooden pins. We are at a loss here, as usual, about dates, and even more than usual. The piece is absolutely in the rough.

No. 613. A cradle of Pennsylvania origin, with stenciled discs and other decorations. One quaint feature here is also the roping of the bottom. We have seen a chair similarly roped. The method is precisely like that used in beds. The stenciling is similar in design to that found on a few small boxes of pine, on one or two "Bible" boxes, and, on a larger scale, on the barn decorations of eastern Pennsylvania, which are to be considerably elaborated in the author's "Pennsylvania Beautiful."

No. 614. An oak cradle with raised panels. The ends of the raised portions of the panels are gouge carved, whereas their sides are handsomely molded. This is a detail we have not previously noted in antique furniture, and we have not yet been able to learn whether similar examples are found abroad. The heavy channel molds or beads on this piece, and the general system of construction, together with the tall foot posts, as purely Gothic as if they were made in the thirteenth century, are features of much interest. These foot posts are in what is called the square turning; that is, the maker did not have a lathe, and he contoured the sides of the square of the post so that it should agree with the outline of a

594. FRAMED MAPLE AND PINE SETTEE. 1720–30.

595. NEW YORK WAGON SEAT. 18th AND 19th CENTURIES.

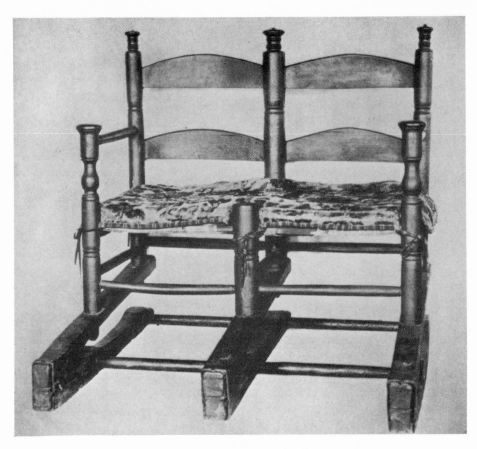

596.   Spring Wagon Seat.   18th and 19th Centuries.

597.   Original Rocker Settle.

turning. The hood of this cradle is somewhat of a puzzle, as we presume it once had a cap, it being cut on the paneled end in the form of a gable. There are a few tacks in the edge of this gable, but no other marks to hint at any attachment of wood. The rockers are neither original, nor are they placed in the proper position. Undoubtedly the posts were extended in the form of legs, and were then bifurcated to receive rockers. We speak thus positively in spite of the appearance of the example to follow.

The cradle is said to have come from Wethersfield, Connecticut, and to date from the time of its settlement, but we have no reliable data. It was bought in Worcester, in 1923.

Size: The posts are $2\frac{3}{8}$ inches by $1\frac{7}{8}$ inches. It is $38\frac{1}{2}$ inches long, 30 inches high, and $16\frac{1}{4}$ inches wide.

No. 615. A cradle, presumably in beech. It is composed of true panels, which are interesting in the construction about the head, formed like five sides of an octagon. The cradle belongs to the Plant family, from the Mill Plain district of the town of Branford, Connecticut, where it is on exhibition in the public library. It has been traced to Jonathan Barker, born 1705. The sides are not quite vertical. The condition is somewhat dilapidated. The rockers seem not to be original. It will be seen, however, that the head and foot posts are turned in the same pattern, and that the head posts, unlike previous examples we have shown, extend above the frame. Of course, this is owing to the manner in which the cap of the hood is attached. The extended and turned posts at the head, however, are a feature of still earlier English cradles.

BEDS

W E HAVE in America no great elaborately turned high posters, such as were found in England at the time of the American settlement. We have records of such beds being ordered from England. Such importations of an ancient period have disappeared. Of course they lack wholly the American feeling, and as we can see such beds in England, the loss is not as great as it might seem at first.

The earliest beds known in America are simple as regards their posts. They are always square in the earliest examples, below the bed rail. Above that rail they may be either square, octagonal or turned, but the turned specimens may be later than the other forms. In every instance the posts taper, and are small. In the square at the frame, the most usual dimension is $2\frac{1}{2}$ inches. We have never seen it exceed $2\frac{3}{4}$ inches on very ancient beds. This dimension continues to the floor without change. Beds turned below the frame are more likely to be of the nineteenth century, especially if the posts are heavy. The Sheraton type, indeed, and sometimes the Hepplewhite, have turned legs. In our period, however, we have not noted an exception to the general rules above. Any delicacy of turning, or any urn turning, means an approach to the end of the eighteenth century. The continuation of a large post to a point near the top is always late and poor, whether it be carved or not.

At the same time it is wholly impossible to assign the plain bed to a date anywhere nearly exact. This arises from the fact that it was in a manner styleless and continued, probably, from 1670 even through the eighteenth century, with practically no change except some slight marks such as we have already mentioned, regarding bolts, etc.

Of course the purpose of the tester and curtains was a double one — to secure privacy, and to shut out drafts. Some of the ancient houses, being the homes of large families, required more than one bed in a room. Indeed, attics, to which the children or the hired men were often consigned, were known not infrequently to have four, and sometimes six beds. It was regarded as effeminate to heat a bedroom for people in health, though for guests or elderly persons the fireplace, almost invariably found small in bedrooms, might be used. It scarcely raised the temperature above freezing. As fashions changed, first the side and foot curtains, and finally the whole top, were dispensed with. In the effort to

598. New York Seat with Spindles.

599. Oak Cradle.

600. Ten Panel Pine Settle. 1710–50.

601–602. Built-in Settle.

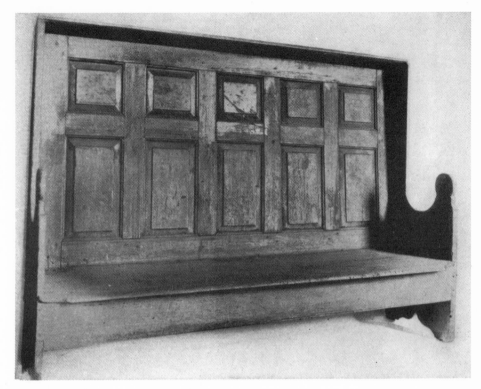

603. TEN PANEL SETTLE. 1730–80.

604. WALNUT PENNSYLVANIA SCROLLED CRADLE. 18th CENTURY.

605. Cradle with Gallery. 1680-1700.

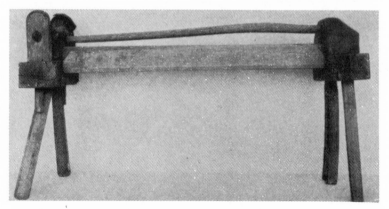

606. Flax Breaker. 18th and 19th Centuries.

ape, rather than to imitate, the ancient fashions, modern beds are put on the market with high posts, but without canopies. This is a makeshift which can scarcely be justified either in logic or taste. If persons desire to have the really ancient beds with canopies, they may omit the lining below the fish-net stitch, and secure a circulation of the air, so that they may still have the old fashion without transgressing sanitary demands.

Some of the old canopies were composed of very rich work, so that the inheritance of a bed, by a special clause in a will, was counted an honor. The bed, with its furniture, a phrase which included everything aside from the woodwork, was the most considerable object of value in the home, even exceeding that of a cupboard.

Nos. 616–618. A four-poster bed formerly in the Hazen house, Haverhill. All the parts of these hangings and the canopy were beautifully laundered and laid away in a box when the bed was purchased. The tester proper was attached on its four sides by laths like old curtain sticks pushed through the open-ended wide hem, and then tautened by straining them over the iron pegs of the tops of the posts.

One sees the trundle-bed head at the foot of the large bed. On the right, in the rear, is a quaint early high chair, and on the left a good New England slat-back.

Why beds are called four-posters is one of the unsolved mysteries, since we can scarcely conceive of beds being constructed without four posts. Perhaps those who gave the name thought of a post only as a high post, and if it was short, called it merely a leg. It is necessary, however, to run one's forehead against one of these posts in the night, fully to appreciate the name.

Of course the only object of the high post was to attach thereto the curtains. In the case of the bed before us, these curtains were held up by strings running from the posts and caught at the centre of the tester in rings. The ordinary method was to tack the curtain to the side lath.

No. 619. A jointed bed, otherwise called a press bed or a slaw bed. These beds were intended to have their heads set in a shallow closet, with two large doors. The bed in the day time was thrown up on the joints of the secondary set of legs, and the doors were closed. The bed is shown without furniture, in order to give an idea of this method of use.

There is an amusing sameness between the needs of the present generation and those of the first generation, in respect to scanty house room. Our remote ancestors, as the family grew large, were hard put to it to provide room for all. Hence we have the scheme of the trundle bed, the settle bed, the press bed, the trestle board, the trammel lamp, the chair table, and various other devices to accommodate many people in a small space.

In fixing the dates of beds it will be observed that in the earlier styles there were no bolts used at the corners, but that the frame was held together merely by the tension of the bed cord. There are two tools, a straining wrench and a special wedge, together, of course, with a mallet, that are used in cording a bed. It is necessary, in case of a new rope especially, to increase the tension of a bed after a few days.

Another detail to be noticed is that the makers sometimes cut a groove into which the rope sank between holes. We are not clear whether this was an improvement or an original plan.

Small beds with low posts got the name "hired men's beds." They were the sort commonly in use for the small chambers.

No. 620–624. A low post bed with a double arch in the headboard, to indicate where grandpa and grandma should sleep. There is also a trundle bed, but without a head. The woven spread shown on the trundle bed seems to have been a great favorite. Multitudes of these spreads still exist, blue being perhaps most preferred.

The bird cage in the remote background is of wicker work, such as was commonly employed in the old days. On the right wall are hanging rope shelves.

No. 625. A trundle bed with a paneled head. Owing to the heavy bar across the head, we consider this an early specimen, but the side bars above the main rails are missing.

No. 626. A bed unique in our experience, sharing in its interest with the settle bed previously shown. Here we have true settle ends, with ogee contours at the feet, but the back of the settle is elongated into high posts. The bed frame hinges on the front of the end boards. When the bed, therefore, is lifted up, as here shown, the counterpane is drawn down over it to cover it. We have purposely exposed the scroll of the settle end to show the arm. The bed is painted blue. It was bought in Worcester in 1923. We know nothing whatever of its age. It is obvious however, from the method of construction, that it was not to be set in a press but to stand free in a room. Of course it could not be used as a settle. At the same time, it is a quaint conceit, and when made up for the night, is of somewhat pleasing outline. At the top there is a shallow frame sustained by a diagonal strut, forming a bracket on each post, over which the coverlet is drawn down.

No. 627. A famous bed, now in the York jail, the Museum in the town of that name in Maine. It is one of the few examples shown in other works. The crewel work and the colors are very rich, especially the greens and reds.   The counterpane and valance are a part of the same work, with uniform colorings, done, of course, on old linen.

A feature giving much flavor to this bed is the use of texts or poems in crewel work, around the upper valance.   The sentiments are such as might appear on samplers.

We are glad to present so clear a picture of this ancient piece, which dates from 1745.   At the jail various details regarding the bed and its donor are preserved.   We are especially glad of the existence of this beautiful example, because it forms a connecting link with the stately beds of the sixteenth century.

Nos. 628–633.   On the left is the only American oak high poster that has come to our attention, or to that of our friends.   It was found in the attic of the Webb House, Wethersfield.   Mr. Welles, who owned the house, when a boy sawed off one of the posts as a ball bat.   Aside from that, the bed is in its original condition, and is an amusing instance of the persistence of the Connecticut taste for oak.   The posts rise in a perfectly plain taper, and the bed is held together by cording only.   When this bed was on the market some years since, the general public entirely overlooked its importance.

In the same picture appears a wing chair made in precisely the same fashion as a settle, except that it has a single seat.   It is of pine, and covered with figured cotton goods.   The chair before the fireplace is of an early turned type.   The chair at the left is of the Dutch turned style, with a kind of stump foot, somewhat later than our period.   Of course the Windsor chair and the stand do not come into our view, but the braided rug and the rag rug go back to a period the beginning of which we are unable to trace.

Nos. 634–636.   Sets of andirons from the George W. Ives Collection.   The Hessian andirons are reversed.   We are informed that if the backs are hollow, the andirons are not very early, and that the original Hessian or other cast type was puddled iron; that is to say, the iron was poured into an open mold and filled in on the back.   The Washington andirons on the other side are of interest.   The middle pair are odd in respect to the so-called square turnings with which the flat members of the posts are tipped.

Nos. 637–639.   A high-post bed in which the posts are made in two sections, the upper part doweling into the lower part, and made detachable.   The upper sections are called poles.   It is possible that the phrase "tent bed," usually describing a round topped bed such as we shall presently show, had some connection with the phrase "bed pole."   It is to be seen here that this bed is turned near the foot.   Its other ornamental details indicate a late date, but the canopy in blue peacocks is very interesting and rather early.

The scrolled-leg chair immediately in front of the lady standing is a good example, as is also the Spanish foot fiddle back chair in the immediate foreground on the right. The ram's horn arms on this chair surpass, in the way of carving, any others we have seen, in respect to the spiraled terminals of the horns.

No. 640–642. A bed with its original canopy of linen. The method of draping the bed, by the use of cords attached to the laths running around the frame, is seen here, also the fashion of attaching the fringe both to the upper valance and to the curtains. The quaint stool at the foot is of the earliest Windsor pattern.

No. 643–645. It would seem that the pudding stick here should be enshrined as a kind of fetish with the Harvard Hasty Pudding Club. The design was worked out in wood probably in imitation of an iron design. The rolling pin in its early form was turned with a knob at one end only. The wooden spoon was common for mixing purposes, as now.

No. 646–649. A folding or jointed six-legged bed, in the George F. Ives Collection. The bracketed head or canopy is quite like that in No. 626. It is designed, as in that case, to hold a screen or coverlet for daytime use, and to be drawn down over the bottom of the bed, whose legs at the foot were jointed if long, or otherwise could shut without folding inside the canopy. A peculiarity of this bed is that there is a jointed frame at the head with a shoe or bottom member connecting the main posts with the secondary set of posts. Further, there was a drawer in this section for bedding. Of course it was available only when the bed was closed, as in the daytime.

We have seen another very handsome bed, something of this sort, in Woodbury, Connecticut. There is also a very pleasing specimen in the rooms of the Dartmouth Historical Society in New Bedford.

The clock at the left is a so called wag-on-the-wall, most of which were imported. It is said that the little chest at the foot of the bed was often used for the extra bedding. The candle stand of wood on straddling legs is a dateless and sometimes styleless article which is nevertheless much sought for.

No. 650–653. A bed in the dwelling in Duxbury, said to have been built by the grandson of John Alden. In this house, though not in this room, but in the bedroom off the kitchen, it is said that John and Priscilla passed the last thirteen years of their life. It is probable that John Alden assisted, by his hand or by his brain, in the framing of this house, supposed to have been built about 1653. Alden was at this time about fifty-three

607. SAMUEL FULLER CRADLE. 1620–50.

608–611. SLENDER POST BED. 18th CENTURY.

612.   SUSPENDED CRADLE.   18th CENTURY.

613.   PENNSYLVANIA DECORATED CRADLE.   18th CENTURY.

614. Oak Cradle, Gouged Carved Panels. 1635–50.

615. Paneled Hood Cradle. 1680–1710.

616–618. CANOPIED BED AND TRUNDLE BED. 18th CENTURY.

619. FOLDING PRESS BED. 18th CENTURY.

years of age. The massive character of the framing and the gun-stock post are shown in the corner through the bed. The bed has upon it a counterpane of the drawn-in candle-wick design, all in white and now so rare. The figures here are not as elaborate as are frequently found. The floral pattern is the most highly thought of. A stool of early but uncertain date and a banister back turned chair, hooked rugs and a braided rug form the remainder of the furniture.

This house is being honorably treated by a Mr. Charles Alden, who has a long lease of it. He is attempting to restore it absolutely on the lines of the original design, and deserves much credit for the wholly new plenishing which he is providing from time to time, as he is able to find suitable examples.

No. 654. A high-post bed in which the chamfering of the posts is quite evident.

Owner: The George F. Ives Collection.

The plainness of the posts in ancient beds is justified by the fact that they are shut in by the curtains. As they were not visible, there was no special reason for working the wood into decorative forms.

In this connection an amusing instance is that of a buyer of an old bed, who indignantly returned it to the seller on the ground that the head posts were plain, and that he would not bear having put off on him a spurious article. The bed was all original. The foot posts were turned, as was the custom in the second period, because they were to be visible. The head posts, on the other hand, being draped, were left plainly octagonal. The bed concerning which the buyer complained was far more valuable, because earlier, than it would have been had all the posts been alike.

CHAIR TABLES

THE chair table, sometimes called when the box is too high to sit upon, a hutch table, is in its best forms a very interesting and important article of furniture. It does not, however, in simple designs seem to appeal strongly to American collectors. It is one of the instances in which fashion has played some part. We show several very important examples. These chair tables were quite common on the New England coast. The appeal to our ancestors of economy in space made chair tables popular, as of course the purpose was to place them against the wall when they were not being used as tables. The oldest specimens have oak frames, but for the most part the frames were maple, or the pieces are mere six-board chests on legs, with table tops of maple or pine.

No. 655. An interesting oval top hutch table in the George F. Ives Collection. The meritorious points are the ogee scrolls on both faces of the legs, and the shoe and stretcher on which they rest. It will be observed that the board which forms the side of the hutch is made on the ends in the form of a single large dovetail, and that there is a lid to the hutch. The cleat, otherwise called a batten, which attaches the parts of the top together, is scrolled so that when the table is used as a chair a decorative feature may appear.

The word "hutch" is not precise in its applications, and has a more general use in England than in America. Even a hutch such as is shown here could be used as a seat with the help of a stool.

No. 656. A remarkable chair table said to have been found in New Jersey. It is of oak, and the top, shown in 657, is scrolled or contoured or shaped, phrases loosely used to denote the same thing, and finished with a thumb-nail mold. The turnings resemble those on two examples of stretcher desks which we have shown, and suggest the William and Mary period. The especial object of importance in this piece is the scrolled X stretcher, a feature we have not elsewhere seen in American chair tables. This example was sold to a museum. It is said that when it was uncrated the finial was missing, and that the piece was therefore rejected. It is all original except the finial, which was constructed by the use of the photograph which showed it before the original finial was lost. The drawer closes flush. The seat is molded like the top. The feet are of the heavy ball type as shown later in a court cup-

620–624. Low, Double Arched Head Bed and Trundle Bed.

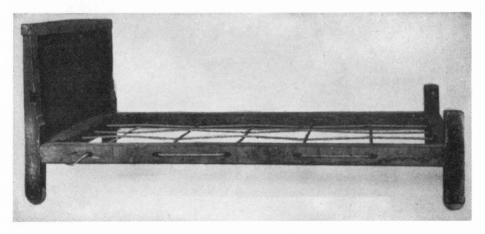

625. Paneled Head Trundle Bed. 18th Century.

626.   Settle End Folding Bed.   18th Century.

board table. It will be noted that the tops of these chair tables are attached with large turned pins, similar to those in the Pennsylvania library tables. The large turnings and the ogee scroll on the skirt or valance provide the finishing touches on a piece of the highest interest. We have not been able to make out the abbreviated legend on the under side of the leaf. Certainly the date is not, as it might appear to be, 1777.

Nos. 658–664. On the left there is a hutch table with a shoe prettily scrolled in the ogee pattern. In the foreground there is a child's wing chair of pine. The back is unusually high and quaint. At the right is a maple chair table with a square oak frame and a drawer, an unusual specimen. In the rear there is a cupboard with a drawer paneled from a solid. In the right foreground is an arch slat back chair of the Pennsylvania type.

This room is one of two which we have seen showing openly the great braces of the frame at the chimney girt. The method of hanging a lantern in the kitchen, as we know was frequently done, is also illustrated.

No. 665. An all pine American Gothic chair table with curved panels in the frame. This piece, which belonged to the author's former collection, he found in the hands of a small dealer in Freeport, Maine. A most astonishing cleat, in the true Gothic pierced form, runs across the top in the dovetailed conventional slot, to prevent warp, and also to avoid the necessity of nailing.

The piece stands upon shoes and the curvature of the panels is obvious. There is a lifting seat. We have never seen another piece of this character, and regard it very highly.

No. 666. A room in the Hazen Garrison house, with many objects appropriate to the date, 1690. A little wing chair, a butterfly table, a straddling high chair, a scrolled pine cradle, a hornbeam barrel, and other features appear.

No. 671. A chair table of the more usual type such as is found in eastern New England. This specimen has gouge carving at the ends of the shoes.

No. 672. A rack formed like a cone. It is designed to hang dipped candles and its construction, it being a homemade affair, is obvious. It is the property of Mrs. De Witt Howe.

TABLES

Persons who have ever camped will have learned the genesis of a table. Some sort of trestle is provided and a board is placed on it. Here, then, is the table as it was used for many ages. In a Greek dwelling of the higher character the table was thus brought to the banqueting apartment and then removed after a meal.

Leonardo Da Vinci's celebrated " Last Supper " shows a board on a trestle of carved shape, but precisely like the ordinary carpenter's horse as to main outlines. The last table known in the Middle Ages was a trestle-board. Early American inventories mention such boards in considerable numbers. They are found in ancient homes in England today. Mr. Bolles found the first one in America at a time when he was probably one of a very small number who would know what it was that he had found. The story of his discovery of it, in an attic where it was necessary to remove some of the structural features to get it out, is one of the epics of collecting.

In the third chapter of *Ivanhoe* one reads how the servants came in and removed the trestle board after a meal. Our ancestors did not feel any special need of fixing the table's top permanently in position, and this is not to be wondered at. With large families it was a convenience to have the long board removed. Of course the trestle-board necessitated a narrow table. The presumption is that the service was from one side, and that the diners did not sit facing one another. The ends of the table were occupied by joint stools, one at each end.

Tables in a fixed form indicate a civilization which has come to a quiet period and believes in stability. A very large table means a great house, with large doors. The first and principal use of tables was for dining. They undoubtedly derive their form from the long tables in the refectories of monasteries. The tables were placed in the parlors as places where conversation was allowed. The long board then adopted in the halls of nobles was required for the great number of retainers. The family of the lord would perhaps have such a table on the dais or raised platform at the end of the hall, at which his family and dependents or guests would sit. His men-at-arms and servants would occupy one or more trestle-boards in the body of the hall. The word " board " is of sufficient explanation of the origin of the table and of our common phrase

627. CANOPIED BED WITH CREWELWORK. 18th CENTURY.

628–633. An Unique American High Poster. 17th or 18th Century.

634–636. Hessian, Square Finial and Washington Andirons.

637–639. Canopied Bed, Sectional Posts. 19th Century.

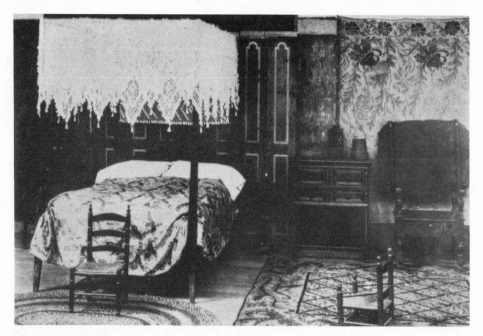

640–642. Canopied Bed with Netting. 18th Century.

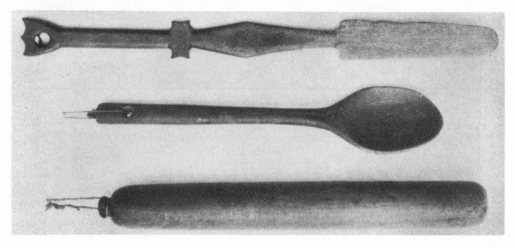

643–645. Hasty Pudding Stick, Spoon and Roller. 18th Century.

" board by the day," and analogous terms. The ancient legal phrase " bed and board " is also referable to the same origin.

The word " table " is pure Latin in origin, and thus etymology enforces the fact of the foreign origin of the table itself. We often forget that the majority of people on earth need no tables. They sit on the floor. A table, therefore, is not the earliest article of furniture, and it naturally comes under the last great division of our book.

The first table designed as a fixture was called a standing table, and was so described in the old inventories. With its great bulbous legs, elaborately turned or carved, it was a ponderous and obvious article in the homes of the wealthy.

As far as we know, none of the great foreign bulbous tables of ancient time is found here. If any such existed in America they have gone the way of the huge beds. The larger an object of furniture, the less likely was it to be imported. The abundance of woods in America stimulated American manufacture and gave freedom to American design. Great tables were precisely what a new country could not afford to import.

It is a curious mark of growth that the first standing tables that we know in this country were made with removable tops. The posts were prolonged, either wholly or in the form of tenons to engage in mortises in the top, which could be lifted off. It was thus convenient to move a table in two parts from one room to another, as the early doors were rather narrow and low.

The table affords rather meagre space for carving. We do not know of an instance of a table leg carved in America. A table frame with much decoration would have interfered with the knees. The table frame was further more or less masked by the overhang of the top, so that it was not a place to encourage carving.

Undoubtedly the introduction of tables with leaves follows naturally from a desire to secure substantially the same results as by the use of a trestle-board, but with less trouble. Thus the gate-legs and the chair tables came in.

Some of the gate-leg tables are intricate and huge, and found in England. The author remembers, when he was a boy, it was the custom in country houses, everywhere to drop the leaves of the dining table, and to set it against the wall between meals. There was no possible reason for it then more than now. It was a continuation of an ancient habit, that is all. We remember one ancient and huge kitchen where two members of the family were left. Invariably the dining table was closed and pushed to the wall after every meal, leaving a great empty space of no possible benefit. Our grandmothers would as soon have thought of leaving the dishes unwashed as of leaving the table in the floor. It is one of the most curious instances of the failure of the human mind.

The trestle style of table survived in small gate-legs sometimes, and also in a few tavern tables, but the tops were in all cases attached. Pins of oak were the ordinary method of securing the tops in position. It was not until the Sheraton time or thereabouts that we have table tops secured by screws from beneath. If we find an old table top nailed down, we may be sure that the nails are not original, although they may be old. We do not remember at this moment having seen an American table with an oak top, although many such may have existed and some may remain. Oak was a very poor material for table tops, especially if one desired a single board. It was inordinately heavy and hard to work. We find pine very early in table tops, imposed on maple frames. We also find maple used to a great extent, although not so much probably in the seventeenth as in the eighteenth century. Maple is a very smooth but very warpy material. Many of the ancient maple table tops are curved like a bow, to a really humorous degree. Incidentally it has been learned that there is no material so good in the manufacture of violins as these warped table tops. Their wood and contour and their age all make them ideal for the purpose.

In the walnut period the entire table was constructed of that wood. The finding of a maple or a pine top on a walnut frame is always suspicious, and generally an evidence that the top is not original.

We cannot too emphatically point out the danger of asserting that a table has its original top. There is no possible method of proving such an assertion about any table. If one removes the top and finds that there is but one set of pin holes in the frame, the probability is strong that the top is original, but if an owner is persuaded that his top is original, he will not remove it to prove the fact. Further, it is entirely possible, by inserting pins, and placing a second top over them, to use the same holes. We have known of instances where old, but not original, tops have been been passed off as original by this method. Pine tops were especially liable to disintegration through wear. We can often be morally certain that the top is original, and oftener still, we can state that there is a strong probability of its being original. Ancient table tops, however, are often found and are easily adaptable to ancient table frames, especially in the case of the tavern table with its one piece top.

Nos. 673–674. The author had the good fortune to discover the table here shown. It was the second trestle-board to be found in America; the first, found by Mr. Bolles, being in the Metropolitan Museum. The main features of such tables clearly appear here. The trestle itself is in

646–649. Folding Bed with Shoe Base and Crane Head.

650–653. Canopied Bed, John Alden House. 18th and 19th Centuries.

654. Canopied Bed. 18th and 19th Centuries.

655. Scrolled Hutch Table, on Shoes. 18th Century.

the form of a double T. Two or three such pieces were connected by a truss along the centre. In the instance before us, there are two spindles, resembling early turned chair spindles, inserted at intervals on the truss, and running to T heads which are in section like the heads of the main trestle. The board is about 25 inches wide. The tops were ten to twelve feet long. The board here is pine. The frame seems to be of maple. The truss was originally held in place by pins run into the post by hand and temporarily holding the table in place.

Owner: Mr. B. A. Behrend.

The table was preserved at the Richardson Tavern, Medway, because Washington had once eaten from it. It was put in the attic, and on the occasion of an auction early in the twentieth century, it was brought out, photographed and sold. Persons from each part of the ancient town, which had been divided, bid on the table. They ran it up above ten dollars, and, the bidder being judged insane by most persons at the auction, it was knocked down to him. The object of the buyer was merely to preserve a Washington relic. No one present knew of the great importance of the piece. The author saw by accident a photograph of the table, and traced it into the West. After an exciting chase and fevered expectancy it was secured. One end of the board is chamfered, while the other end, perhaps, has been cut off a little. In other respects, it is practically in its original condition. It is possible that the tenon of the truss originally ran through and was pinned on the outside, as on the Bolles example. The pins are at present fixed and cut off, and we never sought to withdraw them.

Upon this table there are placed various trenchers of wood and bowls used for mixing or serving food.

It ought to be pointed out that a considerable number of trestle-board tables has been found within a short time, but for the most part, they have been traced to the Shakers, and date around 1800. They sometimes have turned posts. We hear rumors of one or two ancient examples, but we have never seen them.

Nos. 675–676. These illustrations show, on the right, the earliest, and on the left, the next earliest, methods used in America of attaching the sides of drawers to their fronts, in court cupboards or tables. The oak was gouged out so as to get a better hold for the nail driven into the rabbeted end of the front. It thus appears that in this country, at least, the use of nails in drawer construction was earlier than that of the dovetail. The dovetail on the left, one notices, is single. The groove in the side of the drawer is very clearly shown. It engaged a strip of hard wood attached to the inner frame of the table.

No. 677. This table, the property of Mr. George Dudley Seymour, is at the Wadsworth Atheneum, Hartford, and is the only one that we have noticed in this style. It was no doubt suggested through a memory of the trestle table, because its leaves are on the ends instead of on the sides. When these leaves are extended it has quite the trestle-board appearance. It is, therefore, a connecting link between the draw-table and the gate-leg table. The obvious thing for us would be to place leaves at the side of a table.

There is in the rooms of the Connecticut Historical Society at Hartford a table, very massive, its legs being nearly five inches in diameter, which was built as a draw table; that is to say, leaves were drawn out from each end, sustained on elongated cleats, allowing the central portion to drop to their own level. Such tables are known in England, and have of recent years been imported. Lyon illustrates this Connecticut table, which has lost its leaves.

The specimen before us, however, is a modification of that table and an advance upon it, as the leaf attachment is simpler. Most persons who can remember fifty years know that it was a common thing to extend ordinary tables by the use of such leaves with prolonged cleats or tongues, which were thrust into holes cut for them in the table frame immediately under the top. It was a kind of early accommodation answering the purpose of the extension table of modern times.

No. 678. This form of the trestle table, found in a good number of instances in New Jersey, in which the X or so-called stretcher is slightly scrolled, is a good example of its type. One notices, however, that the date is about one hundred years removed from the trestle-board forms we have previously considered.

Owner: Mr. Willoughby Farr of Edgewater, New Jersey.

Nos. 679–680. A pair of trestles and a board about six feet in length, owned by Mr. Harry Long. The ingenious stiffening brace is located at a point where it is wholly out of the way. It is also very effective. It is let down into a slot in the trestles. The two stools are half-moons in shape. The writer does not know their origin.

No. 681. An oak "court cupboard" table. It is, so far, unique in the annals of American collectors. It is reported to have been found in the attic of an ancient house on the North Shore, within a very recent period. It was somewhat fully described in *Antiques*. The author, however, made the illustration here used, before that publication. We have already referred to this table under court cupboards, to show the similarity of the applied turnings to those on such cupboards. This specimen had a drawer at the center, and appears to have one now but only

656.   Oak, Cross Stretcher Chair Table.   1700.

657. CHAIR TABLE WITH TOP DOWN.

658-664. CHAIR TABLES, CHILD'S CHAIRS, ETC.

665.   AMERICAN GOTHIC PANELED PINE CHAIR TABLE.   17th CENTURY.

666–670.   ROOM OF THE PERIOD OF 1700, HAZEN HOUSE.

671.   CHAIR TABLE, 18th CENTURY.

672.   CANDLE RACK.

the front is in place. The drop under the frame was convenient, as far as this central drop is concerned, to serve as a drawer pull.

The top of this table is practically circular. At the present time it is painted in imitation of marble, but we assume that it was earlier in its natural state. The balls of the feet are quite like those in the oak chair table recently discussed. In the present instance they appear to have lost about half their thickness. They are cut down to allow the insertion of casters. In this instance they should be restored, as the elevation of the table and the rounding out of the feet would add very much to its dignity. This table has a subordinate and smaller gate-leg in the rear, on which, when the double top is opened, it rests. There can scarcely be a doubt that this table was made for a room containing a court cupboard, its turnings being so nearly similar.

The diameter of the posts, about $3\frac{1}{2}$ inches, is detailed more fully under turnings. The curious hinges we believe to be original.

It is difficult, of course, to trace the origin of a piece so old. It is not impossible that it came from England along with a court cupboard. It certainly, however, has been in America a very long time, and might easily be American so far as its wood is concerned. It is very curious in this connection that Englishmen tell us that the wood of some of our American pieces is English oak, whereas we are able to point out the error. This statement is not made with any sarcastic intent. We mean only this: that the English, unconsciously, perhaps, wish to establish the English origin of an American piece, whereas we are just as unconsciously leaning to the other side. Those people who absolutely know oak would of course contemptuously brush both contenders aside. This sentence is intended to bear a touch of sarcasm.

Owner: Mr. George B. Furness, Douglaston, Long Island.

Size: $27\frac{1}{2}$ inches high; 36 inches diameter of top.

No. 682. A large table of uncertain use. Probably it was for dining purposes.

Owner: The estate of William G. Erving, M. D. Features of especial interest are the unusual size of the brackets, and the central scroll on the frame, the brackets adding to the strength, and brackets and scroll adding to the appearance. One sees here a medial stretcher rather than the outside longitudinal stretchers.

The tops and rails are pine, the stretcher is ash. The top is $32\frac{3}{4}$ by 64 inches. The frame is $24\frac{1}{2}$ by $54\frac{3}{4}$ inches. The hight is $27\frac{3}{4}$ inches.

No. 683. The table previously described and this type are often called refectory tables. There is a confusion in the American mind between

the refectory and the communion table.   Refectory tables are not known
by that name in the old inventories.   There they were called "long,
standing, jointed."   The term refectory refers to the frequent use of
such tables in college commons, or the like.   It is a somewhat stilted
and un-American word.   A long table would be a better term.   Such
tables are very scarce in America, so much so that when we pass from
those of the type of No. 682, which might be called a long tavern table,
to the communion table, the room between the two for a true refectory
is small.   The communion tables are all too high to be used for dining
tables.   We think it is very much better, therefore, to call them frankly
communion tables.   The table before us was owned by Mr. I. Sack.   We
believe the posts are maple.   The top, as we show it, was of two pine
planks.   We believe it to be a communion table, for if, as we are told,
the fashion in the ancient day was for high tables, why are not the
trestles high?   This table was even higher than it is now, it having had
balls on the feet, which would have given it a hight of about 34 inches.

Nos. 684–686.   We here interpose a picture of a room with cross
stretcher furniture, the greater part of which has already been described,
although the clock on the left, formerly supposed to be of Knickerbocker origin, is now known to be Spanish.   The clock seen through the
doorway has always been known to be English.   We are omitting clocks
from this work, for separate treatment.

No. 687.   A kitchen table with a leaf at the end.

Owner: Mrs. F. Gordon Patterson of Boston.

The brackets stiffening the frame are a feature of merit.   The slide
is missing.

No. 688.   An American all oak square topped table.   It was found
at 59 Central Street, Andover, Massachusetts, in the basement of a very
ancient house, said to be of the seventeenth century.   The table is supposed to have been there for a long time.   There is no possible reason
for regarding it as a communion table, as its shape would be wholly different from what we have been led to expect.

An outstanding feature of the construction is the large bulb upon the
legs.   This turning resembles somewhat the turnings of the one or two
known cross stretcher desks and the cross stretcher chair table already
described.   It is a good deal smaller than the bulb of the Virginian court
cupboard described.   The color and the texture of the oak, the figure of
its beautiful quartering, and the location of the table, so long in one
place, have induced the belief that the piece is American.   This belief
is further reënforced by its style, especially its turning.

The top is made to lift off, small mortises engaging a section of the

673–674. Trestle Board Table with Spindles. Early 17th Century.

675–676. 17th Century Drawer Ends.

677. A Modified American Drawer Table. 1690–1710.

678. X Trestle Table. 1720–50.

679–680. Trestle Table and Stools. 18th Century.

681. UNIQUE TABLE, COURT CUPBOARD STYLE. 1660–80.

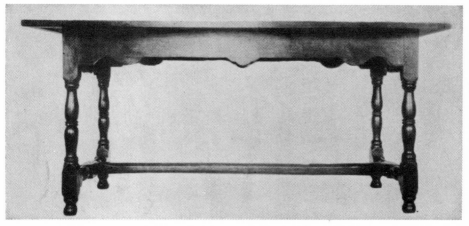

682. MEDIAL STRETCHER TABLE. 1690–1710.

683. COMMUNION TABLE, MAPLE OR BIRCH AND PINE. 1660–90.

684–686. A CROSS STRETCHER ROOM. PERIOD OF 1690.

687. KITCHEN TABLE WITH SLIDE, DROP END, ETC. 18th CENTURY.

legs extended in the form of a tenon. It is thus of the period when the evolution was proceeding from the trestle-board to the standing table. All the boards of the top are apparently from one piece of timber, such is the sameness of the quartering. The method of attaching these boards, seen in No. 689, was through long dowels running from the end cleats into the center of each board. In the passing of time, a shrinkage has made it possible to work these boards much as a swivel blind is worked! The only part of the top that is not original is the wider of the two outside boards. The other restorations are two of the balls of the feet, and two out of twelve of the applied scrolls ornamenting the drops. The brackets are amusingly constructed. On the end next to the post they are thinned into wedge shape, on their backs, so as to be driven into the mortise. The brackets are fastened on the outside and in the usual way, by a nail driven into the frame. The stretchers are molded inside and out.

The interesting method of forming the top, so as to leave no end wood, is obvious. It was of course necessary to nail or pin at the corners of the top. The under side of the top and the inside of the skirt aprons and brackets are hewn and left in the rough. These features of construction belong to the earliest style and throw much light on methods.

Every part of the table is in quartered oak except the legs and the stretchers, and there is a trace of quartering even in them. The fine grain and quiet character of this quartering and its blending from board to board, produces one of the handsomest effects we have ever seen on a piece of ancient furniture.

At this writing we know of no other American table so large and at the same time with as much contrast between the square of the turning, which it will be noted is small, with the large size of the bulb. The hight of this table puts it part way between the ordinary hight and the communion table.

Size: The largest bulb of the leg is $4\frac{1}{8}$ inches in diameter; its square is $2\frac{3}{4}$ inches, scant; its smallest diameter is $1\frac{3}{8}$ inches. The foot is of the same size as the great bulb. The top overhangs about 8 inches, and is $45\frac{1}{2}$ by 46 inches. The hight is $31\frac{1}{2}$.

The authority for the location is Mrs. N. E. Bartlett, whose ancestors have owned the table and from whose house in Andover it came.

No. 690. A long table with brackets and drops.

Owner: Mrs. John Marshall Holcombe. This example was used in the Grant family of East Windsor Hill, Connecticut, as a dining table, before 1700. It was possibly the property of the settler, Matthew

Grant, who was a surveyor, and whose tripod was among the family treasures. The channel mold on the frame is the same as that appearing on American oak chests.

The frame is oak. The style of the turnings is close to the earliest American work.

Size of top: 32¾ by 70 inches; frame, 32 by 58½ inches; hight, 31 inches.

Nos. 691–693. A room containing seventeenth century furniture, or early eighteenth century examples, most of the individual pieces of which are described in this volume. The sheathing is of the character common in houses of that period, but the shutters are somewhat later.

No. 694. A communion table used by the church of Sudbury, Massachusetts, and dated from the second edifice, which was completed and in service in 1655. This table was described in the first edition, but some facts were withheld, since the church did not wish to be annoyed with inquiries. By an arrangement for a fund, the interest of which is to be applied in support of the church, the table was passed into the author's hands. It is, perhaps, the oldest table whose ancestry can be quite precisely traced to so early a period in American history. While not as important from the standpoint of style as No. 698, it is more "in the rough," and, to a certain class of collectors, is of greater interest on this account. We confess to belonging in that class. The original church in the town of Sudbury was in what is now Wayland. When the Sudbury Center church was set off as a new parish, a part of its inheritance from the older association was this table. The top is of yellow pine, and was in one piece. It has been split, but in such a way as obviously to indicate that each section belonged to the original part. It is of pine and an inch and a half in thickness.

Its dimensions are 29 by 84½ inches. The hight of the table is 33¼ inches, from which probably ¾ inch has been lost by attrition and decay. The end overhang is 6½ inches, and the side overhang is 2¾ inches on the front and but ¾ of an inch behind. This indicates that it was intended to show on the side of the wider overhang only. The posts are 3½ inches square. The stretchers are 2 by 2¾ inches. The frame pieces under the top are 3¾ by 1½ inches on the sides, whereas the end pieces are 4 inches wide. The posts extend above the frame ¼ inch and are let into shallow mortise holes in the top to give rigidity and to prevent a sliding of the top. Every part is original.

No. 695. A kneading-trough table. It is in the Metropolitan Museum. There is a drawer and cross stretchers. The front of the drawer carries quaint carvings. The huge wedges which hold the middle truss

688. Square Oak Parlor Table. 1670–90.

689. Quartered Oak Top of Parlor Table.

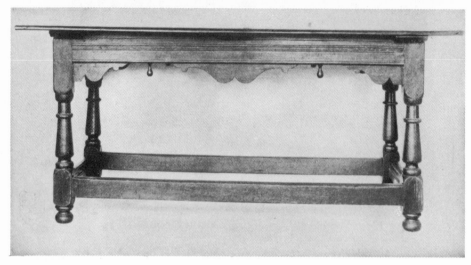

690. Refectory Table, with Brackets and Drops. 1650–80.

691–693. Room of the Period about 1700.

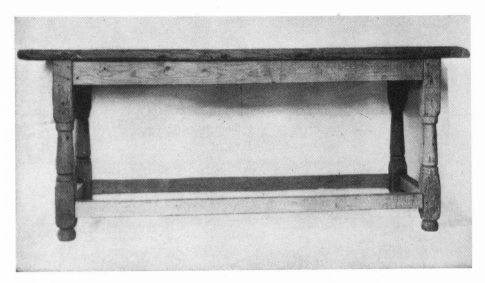

694. Communion Table of White Oak and Pine. 1655.

695. Kneading-Trough Table, X Stretcher. 1700–40.

696. Paneled Frame Table. 17th Century.

697. Light Refectory Table. 1700–30.

in place carry out the sturdy effect of the piece. The cross stretchers are slightly scrolled. So, also, are the straddling legs. The material is pine.

One is naturally prone to the opinion that this piece was a gift constructed by a young husband for his bride. We do not certainly know the origin, but it is probably of Knickerbocker or Jersey derivation.

No. 696. A remarkable table owned by the Metropolitan Museum. It contains a box or hutch below the top, which latter is made to slide, the cleats being dovetailed. The panels are encroached on at the bottom by the base molds of the frame, a thing which we can hardly understand because the table was evidently a thoughtful composition. The turnings are very early and quaint. There is apparently something missing at the bottom, since the flat stretchers were not intended as shoes. Had they been so intended, they would have run under the feet. The top is made with mitered ends to avoid any end wood. It has been thought that the table is American, but we do not feel competent to judge.

It is an odd feature that the only method of gaining access to the hutch is by sliding the top, a thing one would not do with ease, if it were covered with articles.

The top handle of iron is like what we see in English pieces. This table serves to point the statement that early tables were made without leaves. If larger tables were wanted, two or three were put together, and that method continued down through the year 1800. When tables with leaves finally came in, they speedily drove out of use all large tables with one-piece tops. Hence the extreme rarity of such tables.

No. 697. We may name this a light refectory table, as it will do as well as any other term. Still, it is the type of a long tavern table. The objection to using the term tavern table of these large pieces is that they could not, of course, be moved about readily for the use of individuals, a requisite attached to the name and use of the tavern table.

The frame of this table is oak, but the top is pine. There is a good overhang all about, making the table convenient to sit at.

One sees in this table an approach to the gate-leg style of turning. Its plain stretchers, however, hold to the earlier type of the standing table. The plain stretcher was stronger than the turned stretcher, a very important matter if the stretcher was long, as here.

A frame of oak usually points to an earlier date than a maple frame. Still we cannot be too dogmatic on such matters. Old traditions died out slowly in some parts of Connecticut.

Size: The top is 29½ by 67¾ inches. The frame is 20½ by 47 inches. It is 25¼ inches high, and has, obviously, lost something of its feet, which would be proved also by the fact that it is too low to sit at as a dining table.

No. 698. The Salisbury communion table. This very remarkable table, all in American white oak, with carving on the front of the frame, the author saw brought in by the dealer who discovered it. At that time the top was loose, showing the joints between its boards. On the occasion of its sale, the purchaser desired those boards jointed and cleats applied, which was done. Later, when it was resold, a purchaser threw it back upon the seller, on the ground that the top was not original. The inference was natural enough to one who did not know the circumstances.

The table is unique at the time of this writing, in respect to the fact that it is the only American table found with carving on the frame, which also has its original base, practically at the full hight. The table also solves the question whether or not there were ever American tables whose feet terminated in squares, and were not turned. Tables found with square feet in England, we were accustomed to think, had lost the turned feet in most cases. We believe that in some instances the feet were originally square. We did not feel certain that any table of the type existed in America.

The carving consists of interlaced straps, within which are rosettes, technically called a guilloche design. The design is said to be a symbol of eternity. The spandrels are also stippled. As this table stood in front of the pulpit and probably on a dais, elevated at least one step above the hight of the pews, and as the table itself was about five inches higher than a dining table, the carved member was impressively exhibited to the congregation, as they sat. It is for this reason that carving on a communion table was particularly appropriate. The style of the turnings is the earliest American. The only restorations on this table, aside from jointing the top as above mentioned, are the two brackets at the junction of the frame and the posts on the front. Mortised slits in the posts were found, giving the precise width of the original brackets. Broken off nails were found on the frame, showing where the bracket had been nailed in the conventional manner at its inner end against the frame. We were able, therefore, to make a very exact restoration, which greatly increases the beauty and sense of completeness of the table. The construction of the frame is heavily mortised and pinned, there being two pins at every joint on the upper part of the frame. There is a $\frac{3}{4}$ inch mold all around the edges of all the members of the frame, top and bottom. This molding is worked on as in the case of chests, a part of it being done after the frame was assembled.

Size: The top is about $1\frac{1}{8}$ inches thick, $28\frac{3}{4}$ by 89 inches on the surface. The total hight is $34\frac{1}{4}$ inches, this proving that there could not have been balls at the bottoms of the legs. Thirty-four inches is the usual hight for

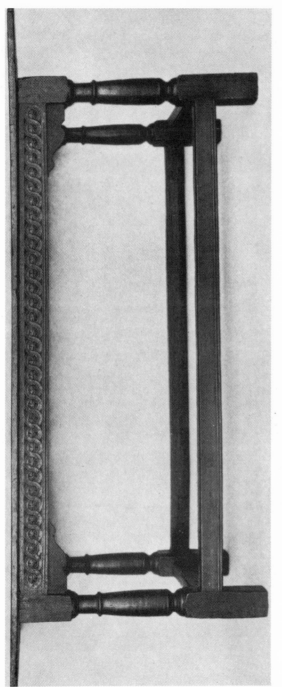

698. Carved Communion Table with Original Feet. 1650–60.

699–700. Sculptured Door Bar, 1778; Coach Horn, 18th Century.

701. WALNUT LIBRARY TABLE. 1700–20.

702. WALNUT LIBRARY TABLE, SCOLLOPED SKIRT. 1700–20.

703. Pennsylvannia Kitchen Table. 1710–50.

704. Walnut Library Table, Bulbous Turned. 1700–30.

705–708. FOUR QUAINT LANTERNS OF VARIOUS DATES.

709–712. KITCHEN OF THE HALE MANSION. EARLY 18th CENTURY FURNITURE.

communion tables so far found. The frame is 26 by 71¼ inches. There is thus an overhang at the ends of about nine inches. The posts are 3½ inches square. The square of the posts at the bottom is 11¼ inches long, six inches of this being below the stretchers. The square of the posts at the top is 7 inches long. The top members of the frame are 4 by 1½ inches. The bottom members are 3 inches deep by 2¼ inches wide.

The restriction of brackets to the front of a table frame is not unusual in smaller tables. In this instance the table was intended to show but one front. There were no mortise holes found in the posts to receive brackets, except at the front.

Nos. 699–700. We are familiar with the wooden door bar, but here is a door bar of iron on which scrolls appear, as well as the initials C. W. and the date 1778. The length is 57 inches. As one sees, this bar is really a huge hasp, the slot of which was slipped over a staple and secured by a pin. The long trumpet below is of the sort used on coaches to announce their approach. It is about five feet long. It requires a man with good lungs and some skill to use it. By adept blowing it gives out a varied musical bar that is very pleasing. Both of these articles were found in Pennsylvania.

No. 701. A walnut library table. This type seems to be found only in the Pennsylvania and Jersey region. These pieces are sometimes called kitchen tables, and their drawers often bear evidence of rough usage. No doubt the type was used in more than one room. The side overhang of these tables, about three inches, is to admit of sitting at either side very comfortably. The tops of these tables are all made removable, by four hand dowels. The overhang at the ends is always generous, and in some cases, more. Examples are found in pine also. If we presume that the pine pieces were for the kitchen and the walnut pieces for the parlor, perhaps no one can show that we are wrong. A characteristic feature is the large size of the knobs. The drawers usually, if not always, overlap, and more often than not they are in different widths in the same frame.

The stretchers sometimes run around the outside and sometimes there is a medial stretcher, as here. As a rule the stretchers are in a square section and not turned, but they are frequently found molded.

Size: The top is 31 by 66 inches; the frame is 25 by 53 inches. The total hight is 29¾ inches. There is the unusual feature of a third drawer.

No. 702. A walnut chair table with a scalloped skirt. Of late, since these tables came into demand, not a few have been found with the scalloped skirt. With the plain skirt, large numbers have been brought into the market.

Such a table as this, not as large as the previous number, might have been used for serving, but as a rule smaller tables of this sort would have been sought for the purpose, and such are found.

Size: The top is $32\frac{3}{4}$ by $48\frac{1}{2}$ inches. The frame is $28\frac{3}{4}$ by $36\frac{1}{2}$ inches. The total hight is $28\frac{3}{4}$ inches.

No. 703. A Pennsylvania table, of which the legs are maple and the other members pine. The drawers are not paired but the knobs are good of the type. The frame is beaded. The posts are $2\frac{1}{8}$ inches square. The stretchers, as usual, are of a rectangular section, but larger vertically than horizontally.

No. 704. A walnut table with scalloped skirt and an end drawer. The turnings are much bolder than usual, approaching almost to the bulbous. The feet are quite characteristic. The table is large and handsome.

Nos. 705–708. A series of four lanterns, the property of Mr. Rudolph P. Pauly. The first example is hexagonal and is of tin, and the second example is octagonal and made of wood. The glasses, however, are divided into two parts with a lead joint. Fascinating little carved finials appear at the angles. This is one of the most interesting and important lanterns we have ever seen. The other pieces are of tin and of ordinary shape, that at the right being probably a sconce from which the reflector seems missing.

Nos. 709–712. The large living room of the Hale Mansion, South Coventry, Connecticut. It was built in 1776, by Deacon Richard Hale, father of Captain Nathan Hale, the "martyr spy" of the Revolutionary War, who was born in an earlier house which was demolished soon after the present house was erected, and which stood but a few rods from it. The maple gate-leg table on the left is one of the daintiest examples. It is very delicately turned and the frame on the end is scrolled. Its top is 41 by $52\frac{1}{2}$ inches, and it is 23 inches high. The table on the right is a very rare specimen called in Connecticut a Windsor table, not from the Windsor chair, but from the town of that name. There is a larger example, which we do not show, in the author's collection. The table shown is of hickory, oak and maple. It was found in Hartford. The oval top is $21\frac{1}{8}$ by $28\frac{1}{4}$ inches, and the hight is 24 inches. The room is well paneled on the fireplace side. A curious little bench stands before the fireplace.

Much credit is due to the owner of the house and contents, Mr. George Dudley Seymour, for the restoration.

No. 713. An extremely rare and important gate-leg example. One of the unusual features is that there are two gates on a side. Another is that there is a leaf on one side only. We may perhaps presume that the table is used in a public place like a court room. There is a good deal of wear shown on the back stretchers and a freedom from wear in front.

713. An Official Single Leaf Gateleg Table.   17th Century.

714. Walnut Table with Four Gates.   1690–1730.

715. WALNUT TABLE WITH FOUR GATES. SOUTHERN STYLE. 18th CENTURY.

716. WALNUT TABLE WITH FOUR GATES. 1690–1730.

717. Gateleg Table. Early 18th Century.

718–719. Gateleg Tables. Early 18th Century.

720. Heavily Turned Gateleg Table of Maple. 1690–1720.

721. Cross Stretcher Gateleg Table. Early 18th Century.

This is proof, since the parts are all original, that the table was used at the ends and back only. The back would not have shown wear had the table been kept against the wall. The nature of the wear would preclude the supposition that the table was used for communion purposes. There is no wear on the rule joint of the leaf, showing that the table was used standing, that is, that the leaf was regularly raised. There is a fine molding on the stretchers, and the stretchers of the gates are molded on all four corners. The front stretcher is chamfered, as clearly seen.

The joint in the front rail is cut on a radius to permit the turning of the leg. There is a legend on the back rail: " Chas. Hosmer, Hartford, Conn." This gentleman has been called the father of the Historical Society in that city. The legend is probably a shipping direction. We are no doubt indebted to him for this splendid specimen, which has now been brought out from the obscurity of a basement, and placed in public view. His date was 1785 to 1871.

The wood of the table is cherry, except the upper frame rail in the back, which is pine, with a molded edge. The legs, as well as the front stretcher, are $3\frac{1}{2}$ inches square. The back stretcher is $2\frac{1}{2}$ by $3\frac{1}{2}$ inches. The table is 78 inches long and 30 inches high.

Our attention has been called, by the kindness of Mr. Lockwood, to the existence of other tables with gates on one side only, which tables were intended for use in pairs, in the same manner as, at a later period, the famous cabinet makers arranged their tables. The specimen before us could hardly have been used in that manner, or the wear would not be found in the portions indicated, although of course we do not know the original intention of the maker.

The massive squares of the legs and the generally large dimensions really give this table a place with the great refectory and communion tables. Nevertheless, the fact that the leaf has a rule joint precludes the naming of a date as early as we would otherwise give.

No. 714.   A four-gate table of walnut.

Owner: Mrs. Lewis Sheldon Welch of New Haven.

The existence of twelve-legged tables, otherwise called four-gate tables, or tables with two gates on a side, has not even been suspected by some collectors. Some six or eight examples are known in America. Possibly the most important is that at the Albany Historical Society, which is the only one that has come to our attention having its gates swing from the centre, and giving a star or raised effect when the gates are all opened. That method of swinging the gate is commoner in England. It is a much wiser design than that of the table before us for, when the gates swing from the centre, the knees of the sitter are not interfered with by the legs of the table.

The origin of the table shown is presumably Connecticut. Of course, the drawer handle is not original. The purpose of using two gates on a side was, of course, the additional stability required by very large tables.

It is important to glance at the question of the probable origin of the walnut used in New England furniture. There is little of clear direct evidence on the subject, but we know that there was a brisk coast trade between the North and the South, and there can be little doubt that Virginia walnut was brought into New York and New England. When we reach Pennsylvania we find there a red walnut closely like the Virginia walnut.

We know that in England walnut was not a commercial wood before the days of Queen Elizabeth, when it was planted under royal patronage to a great extent. When, therefore, the walnut age came in, England was able to use her own forests. She was stimulated to the production of walnut from the fact that it was a fashionable wood in Italy.

Great forests of Virginia walnut, furnishing very fine timber, were found. Of course it was shipped to England, and it would be unreasonable to suppose that it did not also go into New England. It is found in fine furniture here and in New York so frequently that we rest in this conclusion. Nevertheless there were two sorts of walnut native to the North; the black walnut, which is occasionally found in early furniture, and the white walnut, another name for hickory, which of course entered very largely into the Windsor chair and various other manufactures. It is rather misleading to use the term walnut of hickory, because only those specially trained in local appellations will understand the meaning. As a structural wood, the Virginia walnut was superior to our native black walnut, as well as being more fashionable.

The furniture wood of the North is, however, par excellence, maple. The soft maple is the sort most frequently found in furniture. Other names for it are swamp and water maple. It is distinguished from the rock or sugar maple by the fact that the rock maple is a heavier, harder wood, and furnishes even finer material for turning than the soft maple.

No. 715. A four-gate table of walnut. It was found by the writer in Richmond, Virginia, and is now owned by Mr. Chauncey C. Nash. It is somewhat small and low for a four-gate table. The turnings are more characteristic of the South, where we are more likely to find the stretchers in square sections, as here, rather than turned. This table is practically all original except a small mend on the top.

722. SPANISH FOOT GATELEG TABLE. 1690–1720.

723. BOLDLY TURNED GATELEG.

724. Turned Frame Table, Flat Gates. 1790–1810.

725–729. Hominy Mortar, Beehive, Hand Wrought Mortar.

730. Dainty Small Gateleg Table. 1690–1720.

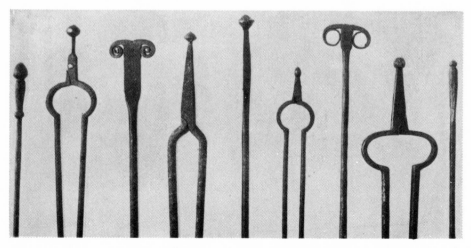

731–739. Styles of Shovel and Tong Heads.

740. SMALL GATELEG, GROOVED JOINT TOP. 1690–1730.

741–742. SPLIT GATELEG TABLES. 1680–1710.

No. 716. A walnut four-gate table found in southern New Hampshire, near Dover.

The top is not original, being of pine as shown. The author has now replaced the top with another of old walnut, in the oval form.

It is thought, where a table has, frankly, a new top, that circumstance detracts very much from its importance. In the instance before us, however, the frame is of great beauty and perfection. We think we have never seen a table with such a forest of legs in so fine a condition, every foot being so nearly intact as not even to suggest restoration.

The effect of these four-gate tables, when opened, in the centre of a room, is startling and impressive as to beauty and dignity. Such pieces are the central objects of the walnut period, more attractive, at least in the author's estimation, than highboys.

The frame of this table is 20 by 51 inches. The hight is 29 inches. As restored, the top is made 70 inches in its largest diameter.

No. 717. A large gate-leg table with unusually fine turnings.

Owner: the Metropolitan Museum. One notices the very long effect of the frame in proportion to the width.

The slot cut in the posts of the swinging legs and in the frame is a distinct blemish in any gate-leg table. It is, however, unavoidable. These tables look best when closed.

Gate-leg tables usually have one drawer reaching about two thirds of the length of the table, and if a table is very large there may be a drawer at either end. In the earliest types there is often under the drawer a central slat on which it slides. We seldom find grooved runs on the drawers of gate-leg tables, their period being rather late for this feature. As a rule, the examples have a beaded member on the frame as seen here. Of course the heavier type afforded more room for ball turnings. If one contrasts these turnings with those of the two tables at the bottom of the same page, he sees less character in the latter.

Nos. 718–719. Two gate-leg tables belonging to the Metropolitan Museum.

In the construction of gate-leg tables, the swing of the leg should not extend beyond the edge of the leaf, nor, indeed, come very close to it. In the example shown at the right, No. 719, the close approach of the gate to the edge of the leaf is an objectionable feature. Of course, the greater the overhang of the leaf, the less interference there is between the human and the table leg. There is a considerable variation in this regard, the overhang ranging from four to six inches.

In determining the source of walnut, we have noted that English walnut has an occasional bluish streak, perhaps every inch or two, running through the grain. All walnuts, however, bleach with wear and washing to a pale gray, especially if they are in an exposed location. The color may easily be restored by the application of a coat of oil. In fact, one is sometimes disagreeably shocked by the great change in color caused by oil.

No. 720. A gate-leg table with somewhat heavy turnings. The wood is maple, including the top. The leaves have the tongue and groove joint, resembling the modern matched board, only less pronounced, and with broader members. This sort of joint is counted the earlier and more desirable, although fine specimens are found with the rule joint, which is denominated by modern cabinet makers a table joint. From the point of appearance the rule joint is better, because when a leaf is down, no opening appears between the leaf and the top.

Claim is often made for great age in the tops of some tables with plain square joints. The burden of proof is on the claimant. We have seen but one or two tables in respect to which it seemed at all likely that the plain joint was ancient.

This table has lost the balls of its feet, but is otherwise original. The pattern of the turning is called the vase and ring, and in this case, taking the center of the turning and proceeding each way from it, it is symmetrical or reversible.

This table is of moderate size, and we shall not annoy the reader with sizes in every case   It is unhappily the very small and very large tables that are most sought for, and those are the examples in which it is more important to note the size. The gate-leg table of medium size is intrinsically as good as its smaller brothers, but sad to say, owing to the innate propensity of a collector to secure the unusual, it is not so much in demand as the small and large examples.

No. 721. A gate-leg table with a cross stretcher.

Owner: Mr. J. H. Stiles, York, Pennsylvania.

We do not remember having seen another example of a stretcher of this kind. The top, we presume, should be oval and not square. Possibly some gate-leg tables had rectangular tops originally, but none such have come to the author's attention.

This table has lost its feet. It has a good ogee scroll on the frame. In this connection we may remember that when this scroll or any decoration on the frame occurs, it of course shows on the end member rather than on the side, which is completely masked when the leaf is closed and largely masked when it is open.

No. 722. A maple gate-leg table with Spanish feet. The top on

743. SMALL WALNUT GATELEG. 1690–1730.

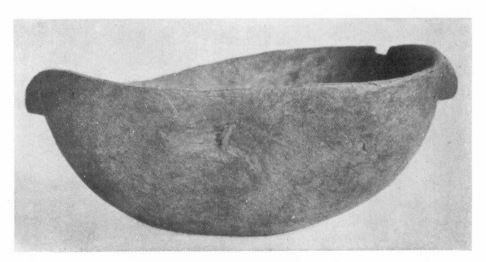

744. HAND-MADE BOWL WITH HANDLES.

745. TUCK-AWAY GATELEG TABLE. 1690–1710.

745A. A FIRE CARRIER.

746. FOLDING GATELEG TABLE. 1700–1730.

747. MAPLE GATELEG.

748. FOLDING GATELEG, GROOVED SCROLLED TRESTLE ENDS. 1690–1710.

749. LONG FOLDING GATELEG. 1690–1710.

this table is of the proper size and has the grooved joint, but it is of pine and of course is not original.

Gate-leg tables with Spanish feet are rare. Some such tables have nearly all the scrolls of their feet new, and in no case have we seen one in which the feet did not require some repairs. The tables go well with Spanish foot chairs in the same room.

Size: The top is 45½ by 47 inches. The frame is 14 by 33 inches. The hight is 27½ inches. There is a drawer.

No. 723. A gate-leg table with heavy turnings In this instance, the stretchers are of a square section. The wood is all walnut. The frame is scrolled at the ends. The construction is without a drawer. All parts are original. There is a grooved joint and the ancient hinges. It is sometimes possible to decide whether a top is new or old by the style of the hinges. The table hinge, as the term is commercially understood now, came in about 1790. Earlier hinges were wrought, their edges being more or less irregular, and often in the butterfly pattern, or if not, in a cruder pattern than the fine hinges of the Sheraton period.

No. 724. A table with flat gates. This style is more generally found in England. Of course, the relation between the gates and the legs of the frame is lost by this method, but it is very early. The turnings here are handsome, and rather unusual. This table is walnut. Square stretchers are the rule with flat gates. It will be seen in this instance that they were beaded on the top and bottom, but that the beading on the top is mostly worn off.

One observes that with the heavy turning it is possible to use the single vase pattern, as here. With a light turning, the vase would be so attenuated as to lose its distinction. Therefore, the smaller the post, the more intricate must be the turning, and the more must it be composed of fine elements in order to retain its decorative features.

Nos. 725–727. A very high vase-shaped hominy mortar with its pestle. On the right is the old-fashioned beehive of straw. It is of the sort seen in the woodcuts in the " Old Farmer's Almanac." These bee-hives were used up to a late period in Pennsylvania, but as they are now prohibited by law, it behooves those who would possess one to be active. The bees, when taking possession of a hive of this sort, will first coat it carefully with wax to make it waterproof. The maker ran two sticks through at right angles to assist the bees in building their comb. Some of the specimens rise to attractive cone shapes. The hight is about 14 inches and the diameter 16 inches.

The owner of these three objects is Mr. Francis Mireau of the Fountain Inn, Doylestown, Pennsylvania.

Nos. 728–729. A huge mortar and a pestle formed by taking advantage of the crook of a limb. The material is apple wood. The peculiar merit of this piece is that while it is brought down to a turned form, the work is carved out by hand, because a section is left in the original size to serve as a handle. The piece is very heavy and large, so much so that probably a common straight pestle would be awkward to operate. This specimen is known to have been used for at least three generations. It was common for persons who were at a distance from a mill in the ancient time to make their own meal in such mortars.

It is owned by the Curtis Inn, Woodbury, Connecticut.

No. 730. A small and very delicately turned gate-leg table all in walnut. The turnings are striped with bands of red paint, which is old, but we suppose not original. The construction is excellent and all original. There is the tongue and groove joint. It will be noticed that on very small tables the walnut top is likely to be considerably less than an inch in thickness, as here. All in all, when the turnings and the size of this table are considered, it is most attractive. It will be observed here that the legs of the gate run to the floor, not only in the outside leg, but in the inside leg. That is, there is a fixed projection below the inside leg, like a leg terminal, though of course it is separated from the upper part of the leg. In this manner the harmony of the table is conserved and its beauty is much enhanced. Old tables are made in both ways, some omitting this complementary feature.

Size: Top, 24½ by 28¾ inches. Hight, 27½ inches. The leaves are 10 inches wide, and the center of the top is 8¾ inches wide.

Nos. 731–739. A series of nine shovel and tong handles. As a rule, the tong handles terminate in a ball. The better designs have a segmental swelled portion, for which there is no use further than the element of design. The best shovel handles are scrolled, as in the third example.

No. 740. A small gate-leg table.

Owner: Mr. G. Winthrop Brown.

It has a drawer and the tongue and groove leaf joint.

The frame of a gate-leg table sometimes, as in this case, is made to take the drawer directly under the top. In other cases, there is a cross member ½ to 1 inch thick, on the frame, above the drawer. This member seems to add strength, but the greater part of the best tables do not have it. We mention the matter because this cross member has been challenged, but we feel certain that it was original in several instances. Of course a drawer very much weakens the frame. It was probably for this

750. CHERRY TRESTLE END GATELEG. 1680–1700.

751–755. TRENCHERS AND UTENSILS.

756. BALL TURNED SPLIT GATELEG. 1690–1730.

757. EARLY MAHOGANY FOLDING GATELEG. 1720–30.

758. A Corner Gateleg. 1690–1710.

759. All Turned Joint Stool or Stool Table. 1680–1700.

760. Birch Frame, Ball and Ring Turned Tavern Table. 1660–80.

761. All Turned Tavern Table. 1690–1710.

reason that a single drawer was used instead of a drawer at each end, on the smaller examples.

Nos. 741–742. The left-hand example has a single drop leaf, which is held up by a split gate; that is, the gate is slit in two longitudinally, in the same manner as the banisters of a chair or the applied spindles on oak furniture. The construction avoids cutting into the frame by a narrower slot. Nevertheless, the table, when open, shows the half leg and is not as attractive as the usual gate-leg form. It is, however, an interesting curiosity and is, as a rule, seen in the smaller tables. It will be observed in this example that there is a triangular frame, but that the stretchers at the base are in the form of a T, and do not run around the table as is usual in the triangular style.

The other example is turned in the knob or ball style, and in other respects opens like No. 741. One is shown open and the other closed in order to illustrate the method of operation.

The left-hand table has a heavy original pine top. The right-hand example is in hard pine, and is reputed to have come from Bilbao. The top is thin, as we often find it in small foreign tables. Nevertheless we see no reason why the table should not have been made in this country, as hard pine was common.

No. 743. An all walnut gate-leg table. All the legs extend to the floor and there is an agreeable wear of the turnings. It is all original except the back leaf, and has the grooved joint. The legs are in a fine state of preservation. The leaves have the fine large original butterfly hinges. The table was found in southern New Hampshire.

Size: Frame, 11 by 29 inches; hight, 28 inches; top, $41\frac{1}{4}$ (with the grain) by $39\frac{1}{2}$ inches. It is an odd instance of a gate-leg table which is actually longer than it is wide! Ordinarily speaking, these tables are larger across the grain; that is, owing to the spread of the leaves, arranged in reference to the swing of the gate leg, the diameter is larger than the length. In this case that is not true.

No. 744. A bowl worked out by hand and in the shape of a cocked hat, or at least to suggest that form. The knobs are left as handles. The material is burl. Of course the object in cutting a bowl from burl was to escape the danger of splitting. The burl is the result of the loss of orderly impulse in a tree. Nature forgets herself and the grain becomes a tangle. The burl is not a knot; neither is it a crotch nor a root. It is a benignant tumor. Such burls are found on the maple, ash, oak and walnut, and probably on other trees.

Owner: Mr. Albert C. Bates of Hartford.

No. 745. A single gate table, otherwise called a tuck-away table.

This example is in maple with a thick pine top, which is chamfered away at the edge below in order to give an effect of lightness, as in the case of the Windsor chair seat. This specimen was found on Cape Cod. One notes the feet of the trestles, cut in an arch from below. These specimens are much sought for and are very rare. They were most convenient as tea tables, carrying out the thought of all the earlier furniture, to provide it in collapsible forms. It will be seen that the stretchers here are turned.

No. 745A. A fire-carrier. These articles, seen from above, somewhat resemble a corn-popper. There are holes in the top so that the coals could be supplied with oxygen. The handle in this instance is cast, but in better patterns it is found wrought. The object was to carry fire from one room to another, or from one dwelling to another. Carrying the fire from one room to another was a quicker and easier method than the use of the spark and tinder.

No. 746. A tuck-away or gate-leg table in which the top swings down so as to present its longer diameter horizontally instead of vertically, as in the instance previously discussed. This table has a history attached to it by a metal plate. It descends from an ancient family. The wood is maple. One notes that the stretchers are not turned.

Size: the top is 20 by 26½ inches — a very small table. The hight is 26¼ inches.

No. 747. A good example of a New England type of the gate-leg table, all in maple. It was in the former collection of the author, and in the Webb House, Wethersfield.

No. 748. A gate-leg table of pine, in which the usual method is reversed; that is to say, we have flat trestles instead of a flat gate. The trestle is crudely carved with an ogee scroll on each side, and it is fluted also.

One notices that the feet must have lost something from wear, as they formerly swept out in a longer curve and formed a more stable base. The flat stretcher, which forms, also, the foundation for the gates, is scrolled. We are unaware whether or not the top is original.

No. 749. A folding gate-leg table. The tuck-away tables are also called folding gate-legs. The term is here applied to trestle-post gate-legs which have a top of a very narrow section.

Owner: The Metropolitan Museum. The shape of the top is against the presumption of originality, as is also the extreme length of the leaf, but we are uncertain on these points. The table is extraordinary, being the longest folding gate-leg we have seen. It may have lost a half-inch at the base, so that the full contour of the shoe forming the foundation of the trestle does not appear.

762. Large Bracket and Drop Table, Original Top. 1670–90.

763. Heavy Small Tavern Table. 1660–70.

764. MEDIAL STRETCHER TAVERN TABLE WITH BRACKETS. 1690–1710.

765. MEDIAL STRETCHER TAVERN TABLE. 1700–20.

766. Heavy High Stretcher Table. 1660–80.

767. Ball Turned Tavern Table, all Legs Raked. 1670–90.

768. MEDIAL STRETCHER TAVERN TABLE. 1700–30.

769. TURNED TABLE. 1700.

770. CROSS STRETCHER TABLE.

Size: The shoe is now 9 inches long and $2\frac{1}{2}$ inches square in the main section. The frame is $35\frac{1}{4}$ inches long. The hight is $27\frac{1}{2}$ inches. The legs are $1\frac{5}{8}$ inches square. The top of the stretcher is $5\frac{5}{8}$ inches from the floor. The center board of the top is only $6\frac{1}{2}$ inches wide, and its length is 43 inches. The leaves are each $10\frac{1}{2}$ inches wide. The thickness of the top is only $\frac{3}{4}$ of an inch.

No. 750. A heavy trestle gate-leg. The wood is cherry. It is all original with the exception of a very small section of one leaf, shown at the joint in the picture. This is an early example of the use of cherry. It would not have been necessary to have slotted the base for the flat gate, but so we find it. It would seem that the flat gate was sometimes used in order to avoid cutting out sections of the frame at top and bottom. The shoes are pretty well worn down on their uppers, as one might say! They were once scrolled with a cupid's bow; that is to say, a double ogee curve. They probably have lost about an inch. The joint is grooved.

Size: The top and the flat gates are $\frac{3}{4}$ inch thick. This is usual in small tables of hard wood. The posts are "stocky" for so small a table, being $2\frac{5}{8}$ inches, flush, square. The thickness of the table, closed, is about $15\frac{1}{4}$ inches; the leaves are $17\frac{1}{8}$ inches wide; and the length is 36 inches. Thus the oval is extreme, and it is considered in good style on this account.

Nos. 751–755. Three shallow vessels of burl. The little instruments between the bowls are Indian tools consisting of minute parallel knives for stripping up wood for basket work.

Owner: Mr. Albert C. Bates, Hartford.

No. 756. A gate-leg table with ball turnings and with two split gates. The material is yellow pine or, as some would say, piñon.

The turnings are very bold and interesting, but the members of the lower frame appear rather lean, as is frequently the case in tables of this kind.

No. 757. A folding gate-leg table of walnut. It originated in the South. The leaf has the rule joint. It is impossible to determine precisely when this type of joint came into use, but we find it well established by 1750.

This example is very compact, the thickness of the table when folded being only $6\frac{1}{4}$ inches. The top is 35 inches long and $42\frac{3}{4}$ inches wide — a very strong oval. The top has a fine thumb-nail molding. The hight is $24\frac{1}{2}$ inches. The piece has good style, with a long overhang and a large top in proportion to the base.

No. 758. A corner gate-leg table, with a triangular frame and a top which is square when opened, and in the form of two triangles when closed.

Owner: The George F. Ives Collection.

We have seen another table with a base precisely like this. The top had been restored in a round form.

Size: The top is 31 inches square and the hight is 27 inches.

Tables of this sort are important and attractive.

No. 759. With some hesitancy we insert this table at this point, at the end of the discussion of gate-leg tables. We may call this piece a stool or a table or, better yet, we may use the term stool-table. It was bought in Portland, Maine. All the legs are on a rake and not merely two, as is usual. All the members are turned. The condition is fine. The top is pinned on in four places at the center of each side, and the pin runs entirely through the frame. All parts are of maple.

The size of the frame at the stretchers is $13\frac{1}{2}$ by $16\frac{1}{2}$ inches.

The modern paint has now been washed off, and without the application of anything whatever, even of wax, the wood has a beautiful appearance.

771.   HEAVY TAVERN TABLE.   1680–90.

772.   HEAVY TAVERN TABLE.   1660–80.

773. Oak and Pine Tavern Table. 1690–1700.

774. Small Oak Tavern Table. 1670–90.

775. High Stretcher Tavern Table. 1680–1700.

776. Walnut Table. 1690–1700.

777. Walnut Table. 1700–30.

778. SCROLLED SKIRT TAVERN TABLE. 1670–90.

779. HEAVY OAK TAVERN TABLE. 1660–90.

TAVERN TABLES

W E NOW enter upon the discussion of the tavern table, about which something has already been said. In brief, we may state that it is always small, and was always, probably, originally without a leaf. It was designed to be moved about as wanted, especially in taverns, to serve guests wherever they happened to be sitting. Vast numbers of these tables existed, and a good many of them remain today.

No. 760. This ancient example of a tavern table has a frame which we think is birch. There are heavy turnings in the ball pattern, with incipient rings. It will be seen that the side stretchers are high, for what purpose no one has discovered. They are in the way of a person's legs. The only manner in which the table could be comfortably used was to sit at its end.

Owner: It was in the collection of Mr. B. A. Behrend.

Only the feet are restored. It was found in Milford, Massachusetts, in 1917. The top has a very long overhang, 17 inches or more.

The bases of these tables are usually in maple, and their tops are almost invariably in pine, sometimes yellow and sometimes white.

No. 761. A tavern table with rather meagre turnings, as is usual in the small types. Of course it was thus easier for the maids to move about.

No. 762. This handsome heavily turned table with brackets and drops, with its rare and original top, should perhaps not be classed among tavern tables. We have, however, a table a little too large for the tavern table and perhaps large enough for a breakfast table, but not for a dining table.

Owner: Mrs. G. C. Bryant, Ansonia, Connecticut.

One should compare this table with the heavy type preceding it in this book. There is an astonishing similarity between the brackets of these tables. The author has seen certainly a dozen, and perhaps twice as many, in which the brackets had practically the same contour, although some are slightly elongated to accommodate themselves to the length of the frame to which they are to be affixed. They are set into a thin mortise on the post, and attached to the frame below at their inside end by nails.

No. 763. A small, heavy tavern table.

Owner: Mr. H. W. Erving.

The frame is oak. The turnings are very early, and should be compared with those on the Robinson chair.

The size of the frame at the top is $14\frac{3}{4}$ by $8\frac{3}{4}$ inches, and it stands 21 inches high with the feet missing.

No. 764. A tavern table in which the stretchers are turned and a medial stretcher does duty for the two which would otherwise exist, one on either side of the table. There is an advantage in this method of construction, inasmuch as the posts are thus mortised in one direction only, and are left stronger. There is also a gain, to some minds, of an esthetic nature. This example is shown to have brackets worked upon the members of the frame, rather than applied. This method is carried around three sides of the table, but the back member of the frame is plain. The turnings are good. A portion of the feet is lost. The frame is maple, and the top is pine, and we believe original, though the drawer is renewed, and it would have been better with a knob of wood.

Size: Frame, 21 by 31 inches; top, $27\frac{3}{4}$ by $40\frac{5}{8}$ inches. Hight, $25\frac{1}{4}$ inches.

No. 765. A small tavern table with old black paint. It is all original.

No. 766. A rarely good tavern table belonging to the Metropolitan Museum. Its turnings are in the knob or ball style, and it has the distinction of well shaped brackets under the frame, and of high stretchers and a medial stretcher. We presume that there were drops. The top is so large that it comes under the class, as does Mrs. Bryant's table, of a breakfast or small dining table.

Size: The frame is $23\frac{7}{8}$ by $18\frac{1}{4}$ inches. The top is $36\frac{3}{8}$ by $36\frac{3}{4}$ inches, intended, of course, to be square. The square of the leg is $2\frac{1}{2}$ inches. The hight is $26\frac{1}{2}$ inches. There is a 4-inch drawer. It is $12\frac{1}{4}$ inches to the top of the high stretcher, and $4\frac{1}{2}$ inches to the top of the medial stretcher. This class of tables is, when we consider both date and style, the next most important to the refectory tables. Fine examples of this type are better than moderately good examples of the refectory type. This example lacks no feature counted strong and important.

No. 767. A tavern table belonging to Mr. Chauncey C. Nash. We count it of no small importance. All the legs are raked. The turnings of the stretchers are in the ball pattern. It has a wide overhang at the ends.

No. 768. An all turned tavern table with a medial stretcher. It is all original, unfinished, and lacks only a little of the feet. The drawer has an overlap, hence the date is not so early as the tables with the flush drawer.

780. Maple and Pine Tavern Table. 1700–20.

781–2. Stand and Pewter.

783–4. Stand and Hat Box.

785. ALL TURNED SCROLLED TAVERN TABLE. 1690–1710.

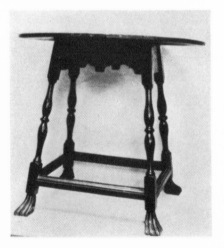

786. SPANISH FOOT TABLE. 1690–1710.

787. HIGH STRETCHER TABLE. 1680–1700.

No. 769. A little cherry table from Pennsylvania. Although so light and delicate, the drawer has the early side run which establishes a date of about 1700 or a little earlier.

Owner: Mr. L. G. Myers.

Size: 25 by 16½ inches. It is 27½ inches high.

No. 770. A walnut table from Pennsylvania. It has the rare and interesting feature of an X stretcher. The top is round. It is 29 inches in diameter. The hight is also 29 inches; very unusual for so small a table.

Owner: Mr. L. G. Myers.

No. 771. A heavy tavern table in walnut. The large cup turning is striking. It appears on one or two gate-leg tables. This example is too heavy for a tavern table, and most probably was used at the side of a dining room. There is the so-called stone mold on the upper members of the frame. The legs are massive and the drawer is on grooved runs.

Owner: The estate of William G. Erving, M. D.

Size: The top is 29 by 41¾ inches. The frame is 21 by 32 inches; the hight is 28 inches.

No. 772. A table resembling in its turnings and brackets No. 762. The posts are heavy, as in the early type, and the piece is, like the preceding, too massive to be moved about often. It lacks the cleats on the top, which is original, and measures 39¼ by 41 inches. The hight is 29 inches.

Owner: Mrs. J. Insley Blair.

No. 773. A tavern table with an oak frame and pine top. It is wholly original and never had a drawer.

Size: Frame, 20½ by 30½ inches; top, 26 by 40¼ inches; hight, 26½ inches.

No. 774. A small oak stand or table, the top of which is old but not original, and the feet of which are lost. It has, however, a fine sturdiness and a style of turning quite like that of the very earliest examples, as seen in the Salisbury communion table.

Size: Frame at the top, 17⅞ by 8⅝ inches. The top is 25 by 18¼ inches. The hight is now 22¾ inches, to which we should probably add 2½ inches to obtain the original hight.

No. 775. A walnut high stretcher tavern table.

Owner: Mrs. J. Insley Blair.

The top is also of walnut. The small size and striking turnings of this table render it very attractive. The turnings here are not the usual ball or knob sort, but the balls are separated by a considerable distance. The turned stretchers are most interesting.

No. 776. An all walnut table, all the legs of which rake. The meritorious brackets and corresponding central ornaments on this table, together with the delicacy of the turnings, afford a very satisfactory and complete result. Every part is original. There were never drops on the frame, there being scarcely space to receive them.

Size: The frame at the top is $10\frac{1}{2}$ by $17\frac{1}{4}$ inches. Just below the stretchers it is $18\frac{1}{2}$ by $21\frac{1}{2}$ inches. The top is $27\frac{3}{4}$ by $32\frac{1}{2}$ inches. The stretchers are very strongly molded for half their hight in a cyma scroll, usually called a stone mold. We do not know the origin of the table, but it was purchased in Boston in 1923.

No. 777. A small walnut table originating in Pennsylvania. On the drawer there is a crude scratch inlay, a scroll filled in with a white wood, none of which shows in the picture.

No. 778. An early tavern table with an oak frame. Although it has lost its feet, the molding on the frame and the brackets, and the early type of the turnings, make it interesting.

No. 779. A heavily turned tavern table of very early date. It was not the custom to use brackets on the smallest tavern tables, even when their style was otherwise counted good. In this example the frame is molded, and, above and below, the stretchers are marked by a double bead. The frame is oak. The top is pine. All parts are original.

Size: The frame at the top is $10\frac{1}{2}$ by $22\frac{1}{4}$ inches. Just below the stretchers the size is 14 by $22\frac{1}{4}$ inches, by which it appears that the splay of the legs is in one direction only. The size of the top is 20 by 34 inches.

This table originated near Greenfield. It was found by Dr. Miner.

No. 780. A tavern table with maple frame and pine top. The turnings are especially good. All parts are original. The drawer, as it appears, is not flush. A stretcher desk in this work has very similar turnings.

Size of the frame: $17\frac{5}{8}$ by $24\frac{5}{8}$ inches. The top is $23\frac{3}{4}$ by $37\frac{1}{2}$ inches. The hight is 25 inches.

Nos. 781–782. A stand or small tavern table. It is difficult to draw the line between the tavern table and the stand, just as it is difficult to draw it between the tavern table and the small dining table. We could make a division according to size, but it would be purely arbitrary. Curiously, the name stand seems not to appear in the early inventories. Table was made to do service for stand. We find standard very rarely, but its meaning is not the same as stand. We fail, in the published inventories at this time, to find a wash stand.

A discussion as to what was used for a wash stand cannot be dismissed by the flippant " they did not wash." Small tables like this were used, or larger tavern tables. We believe that there was no wash stand, so called or so designed, in the seventeenth century in America.

The pewter articles upon this piece do not belong to our subject. The wash-bowl and pitcher, generally in use, were of pewter, or, perhaps, sometimes of brass. We have an instance when visitors at a house of some pretensions washed at the pump.

This piece is from the collection of Mr. B. A. Behrend.

Date: about 1700 to 1781.

Nos. 783–784. A small, neatly-turned tavern table in black. It is all original.

The size of the frame is $14\frac{1}{2}$ by $20\frac{1}{2}$ inches, and the size of the top is $17\frac{3}{4}$ by 27 inches.

The box is intended for a hat. We have been informed that such boxes, in wood, with a handle snapping on somewhat like a blind fastener, are found in Sweden. This box was bought in America and we do not know its origin.

Date: about 1700.

No. 785. A tavern table turned with much delicacy. It has the additional merit that it is not only scalloped on the sides, but on the ends of the frame, and has a drawer. Enough of the balls of the feet remain to show what the contour was. We are always pleased to see so much legitimate wear on the stretchers. The reader's attention is called to the use of the word legitimate!

No. 786. A tavern table all the legs of which rake and terminate in Spanish feet. There has been much discussion as to the appropriateness of carving a Spanish foot in a slanting position. We believe that this table is, to the time of present knowledge, unique. It is certainly most interesting.

It is in the possession of Mr. I. Sack.

In dating a piece of this character we are of course governed wholly by the feet. The date is from 1690 to 1720.

No. 787. A high stretcher table, the skirt of which is scalloped. The ball turning is always distinctive. The frame is maple and the top pine. The date is about 1680 to 1690.

Size: The top is $28\frac{1}{2}$ by $37\frac{1}{2}$ inches — a very wide top. The great width in proportion to the length was probably intended to make a roomy table for four persons. One notes the odd absence of any medial lower stretcher.

No. 788. In this example we have a detail of style which, so far, is new in our description. This table is called a trestle tavern table. It is built in the fashion of the trestle table, with a tapering shoe corresponding to a tapering cleat above. The lower stretcher is turned to correspond with the posts, but the upper stretcher is a plain member. The frame is maple and the top is pine. This piece is altogether original and unrestored. It was found in Connecticut. The convenience of such tables, without any frame below the top, is quite obvious. They could be drawn close to the user. They were available as stands or tap room tables, or for any purpose where a light piece was required. The analogy of this table to the extremely early table board and trestle is at once suggested, and the pattern was no doubt derived from that source.

Size: Top, in one piece, $18\frac{1}{2}$ by 30 inches. The shoes are $15\frac{1}{2}$ inches long. The hight is $25\frac{1}{4}$ inches.

No. 789. A stand or small oval tavern table, painted black. It is all original. The frame just under the stretcher measures $12\frac{1}{2}$ by $15\frac{1}{2}$ inches. The oval top is $21\frac{1}{2}$ by 24 inches. The hight is 23 inches.

Date: 1680 to 1700.

No. 790. A stand in which all parts are original except the top. It is too small to be called a tavern table. All the legs rake and are neatly turned to correspond with the stretchers. One notices the cutting of the frame in the form of a bracket, which is one with the frame. We presume that the top is two or three inches too small in diameter. The frame of this little stand is exactly square.

No. 791. A trestle tavern table belonging to Dr. Mark Miner of Greenfield. It differs slightly from the table already figured, in having the upper as well as the lower stretcher turned. It is noted also that the shoes are wider than the square of the post.

Nos. 792–798. Wooden utensils for the table, together with a goffering iron. The smaller trencher in the foreground is a humorous example. The author remembers, when a boy, going on one occasion to a farmhouse for dinner where, after the meat course, the family, following the example of the head of the household, all turned their plates bottom up and received their pie on the new surface. Do not, gentle reader, criticize the neatness of this proceeding! Our ancestors were told to " lick the platter clean." This little trencher is frankly built to be used on both sides, being hollowed unmistakably for that purpose.

The large trencher just behind it is precisely in the shape of a modern soup plate, and is the finest piece of the kind that we have met with. The other pieces with covers may be called tankards or any one of various other names. The left hand piece is prettily inlaid in a diamond outline of white wood. It will be seen that in both instances one of the staves is made very narrow and so shaped as to provide a handle. The

788. Trestle Frame Tavern Table. 1670–90

789. Small Tavern Table. 1700–30

790. All Turned Stand. 1690–1700

791. Trestle Tavern Table. 1670–90.

792–98. Flounce Iron, Trenchers and Noggins.

goffering iron is cast and set on a brass standard. One heated the removable interior and then, thrusting it into the pod, secured a rounded surface for ironing the flounces and furbelows of that generation.

No. 799. An oval stand or small tavern table with all legs raking. It is of maple and belongs to Mr. Edward C. Wheeler, Jr.

Size: The top is 18¾ by 25¼ inches. The hight is 21⅜ inches.

No. 800. A table with a triangular frame and a circular top. The cabinet work of a triangular table was more difficult than that on a square frame. Such a piece, however, has esthetic uses and, practically, the long segment of a side affords a greater overhang than is usually found in small tables. Such tables as a rule have no drawers.

Owner: Mr. Chauncey C. Nash.

Size: 28¾ inches in diameter of top. Hight, 25 inches.

The date is about 1700.

No. 801. A triangular table frame with raked legs. This is a light example, the property, with its furniture, of Mr. B. A. Behrend. One sees hanging from the edge a double bowled Betty lamp, the lower section being built to catch the drip of the upper part. There is, above, a candle stick with a curious handle which would allow it to be hung on a hook as a sconce. The other piece is a sand glass. The date of the table is about 1700–1720.

No. 805. A larger and heavier triangular table with the round top. It was in the author's former collection. It is all original. In many cases feet have to be restored. Of course, the advantage of raking the legs was found in increased stability. One sees that the stretchers are molded, as is also the frame.

Nos. 806–808. We have our first example of the adjustable candle stands. The arrangement by which the central shaft could be lifted was a ratchet and pawl. The base is a large block of wood made frankly in this shape to secure stability. The candles were of course placed at the ends of the crossbar. The lower standard is of pottery, from Virginia. It is of red clay with a coarse black glaze, and is from the old pottery, formerly at Morgantown, now West Virginia. It is similar in texture to the folk pottery of New England and Pennsylvania. These three articles are the property of Mr. H. W. Erving.

No. 809. This is a very quaint ratchet candle stand on stick legs. The candle is set immediately on top of the small shaft.

Owner: Mrs. J. Insley Blair.

No. 810. A stand of delicate turning and a series of ogee scrolls. The drawer is false, and the knob is original, the table never having had a drawer. While this stand boasts no remarkable feature as a whole, it is very attractive, being quite perfect, and in maple, the wood we best love for such purposes.

Owner: Mr. Edward C. Wheeler, Jr.

Size: The top is 16 by 25 inches, and the hight is 24½ inches.

Nos. 811–814. In the first of these reproductions we show two iron latches. Plate latches with springs were in use from about the year 1740 down to 1790. As a matter of fact they are found in use for the simpler rooms of many fine dwellings.

No. 812 is a little candle stand with a heavy X base and with candle bar in the form of balls. A third candle was set on the top of the shaft.

No. 813 is a small embroidery frame. There is a very perfect universal joint, or ball and socket joint, as it is sometimes called, with a wooden screw to set it. The feet are attached like the legs of a Windsor stool. The frame could be swung at any angle toward the operator, and the hands could reach under the piece to be embroidered, which was placed over the frame, previously covered, as we have seen, with cloth; and another hoop was placed over it to hold it taut.

No. 814. The most interesting of all the pipe tongs which have come to our attention. They are made in a square section and not round, as are several of the other similiar examples. The shape of the scroll and of the thumb piece for pressing down the tobacco, and of the nail which was a guide for the cleaner for the bowl, are all clearly shown. The tongs bear on their side a legend stating that they were captured at Fort William Henry. They are shown here as they hung in the old Williams House, South Easton, Massachusetts. They are understood to belong now, by inheritance, to Mr. Fred H. Williams of Boston.

No. 815. An oval maple stand.

Owner: Mr. Edward C. Wheeler, Jr.

Size: The top is 18¾ by 27¾ inches. The hight now is 20¾ inches, to which we should add some two or three inches for the feet, which are lost. The turnings are delicate. One sees in this table the usual cleat which runs across the frame of oval tavern tables, and is set its full size into the frame. It is to prevent the breaking off of the edge of the top, and is very necessary. The heavy stretchers are plainly early.

No. 816. A burl bowl, remarkable for its size, although there are larger; but more remarkable for its shape, worked out by hand. The burl often grew so large that the side of it next the tree was of a hollowed section. The maker of this piece took advantage of that fact to carve ears.

The wood is probably maple, though others in the author's possession,

799. SPLAYED TAVERN TABLE. 1680–1700.

800. TRIANGULAR TABLE. 1690–1710.

801–4. RAKED TRIANGLE TABLE.

805. Heavy Triangular Table. 1720–1740.

806–809. Ratchet and Pottery Stands.

810. Maple Table with False Drawer. 1690–1720.

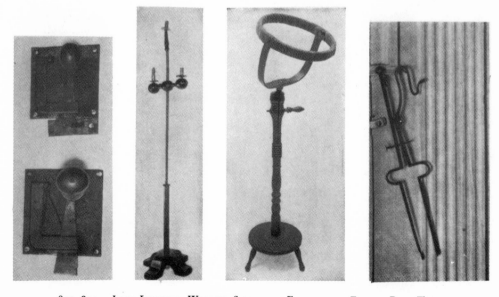

811–814. Iron Latches, Wooden Standard, Embroidery Frame, Pipe Tongs.

815. OVAL MAPLE TABLE. 1690–1710.

816. GREAT BURL WROUGHT BOWL WITH EARS.

with nearly the same figure, are pronounced ash by such good judges of wood as Mr. Henry Ford.

The diameter of this piece is 23 inches.

Mr. Luke Vincent Lockwood has a bowl, turned, of a diameter of about 29 inches, from the author's former collection. These are the largest we have found. A few years since, these bowls were knocked about as encumbrances. The author found the largest specimen at a shop conducted by a person notorious for getting the full value for his goods; nevertheless, he was willing to be rid of the bowl at a ridiculously small figure. Those were the happy days!

No. 817. We have previously shown several tavern tables with high stretchers corresponding in design to the medial low stretcher. In the example before us, we have a very aristocratic specimen. In addition to the usual ball turning, it has at the centre of the turning a double vase motive. A molding carried about the frame is another refinement. The skirt or valance, as it is indifferently called, on the frame, is cut in very handsome brackets and scrolls. The drawer is provided with the side grooves.

This table is from the Prouty Collection, and has been previously illustrated.

Nos. 818–820. A remarkable, and as far as we have learned, unique set of hardware in the tulip-bud pattern. In a decorated chest of drawers shown we have a tulip-bud of precisely the same contour as that which is here wrought in iron. The scroll of the latch-bar is a large spiral. The bar, indeed, is altogether the most remarkable we have ever seen. We see here for the first time that, in the best early hardware, there was a purpose to match the hinges with the latch, carrying the same motive through all.

We are not aware that attention has previously been called to the matching of the design of latch and hinge.

No. 821. A high stretcher tavern table with ball turning and pierced brackets. This fine example is practically all original. It is the property of Mr. Chauncey C. Nash.

While a trifle simpler in some respects than the example preceding it, this table has the unusual feature of the pierced bracket. As an amusing instance of the rapid increase of appreciation in such a piece of furniture, we may say that this table, as soon as found, changed hands five times in five days, the owners being in three states. It has since been sold twice. Were it supposed to be on the market, undoubtedly buyers would stand like dogs at a woodchuck hole for an opportunity to seize it.

In this connection, we have an opening to answer the question so often asked, why there are so many antiques. The answer is to be found in the death of collectors and the consequent dispersal of their treasures. It is also to be found in the occasional financial embarrassment of collectors, for they are not all millionaires. Some of us have court cupboard tastes and pine cupboard pocketbooks. Another explanation is to be found in the unwisdom of collectors, which often permits them to resign pieces whose importance they are not keen enough to know. While this is an unusual circumstance, it is more apt to occur in the case of the more important pieces, as in that of some we could mention, but, frankly, we would not dare. Again, dealers sell, the small to the great, and so the process goes on, until at last, little by little, such things are caught in the drag net of the museums. But be it understood they are not bought by the museums, who either never have funds for such a purpose, or, if they possess the funds, they lack the quickness to seize their opportunities. They achieve their greatness through the gifts of their friends.

Thus, through the reasons we have mentioned, and by sickness and by accident, and by cupidity, the same piece sometimes comes often into the market. In this manner one of the best articles known has changed hands nine times in four years.

No. 822. A beautiful and rarely outlined little table belonging to the estate of George F. Ives. Except for the loss of its feet, it is in fine condition. The turnings are bold for so small a piece, the stretchers beautifully agreeing with the legs. The scrolls on the frame are different on the legs and on the side. The narrowness of the frame and the depth of the scrolls forbade a drawer.

No. 823. A walnut table.

Owner: Mr. Edward C. Wheeler, Jr.

The frame is scrolled, and we find a molding run about it, adding to its importance. Though the feet are missing, the bottom stretchers still stand up well from the floor. The turning resembles that of No. 817, and the scrolling on the skirt is slightly suggestive of that, as is also the molding. One can see from that example how the feet of this appeared.

Size: The top is $13\frac{3}{4}$ by $23\frac{3}{4}$ inches, and the hight is 25 inches. Probably, in modern phrase, the table would be called a stand.

No. 824. A bobbin reel. We moderners should distinguish between this and the spinning wheel. It was merely to wind the bobbins for the loom, and was used in the seventeenth and eighteenth centuries.

No. 825. A small table with a square frame and an octagonal top. The piece is very perfect and has neither been tampered with nor restored, nor does it require it. The paint, however, might be washed off, as it shows now in two colors. The points of merit are the boldly scrolled, though simply shaped skirt, and the unusual shape of the top. There is

817. HIGH STRETCHER SCROLLED SKIRT TAVERN TABLE. 1680–90.

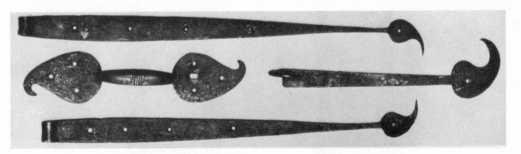

818–820. AN UNIQUE TULIP BUD DOOR SET. 18th CENTURY.

821. High Stretcher, Pierced Bracket Tavern Table. 1680–90.

822. All Turned Scrolled Skirt Tavern Table. 1690–1710.

823. High Stretcher, Scrolled Skirt Tavern Table. 1690–1700.

824. Bobbin Wheel. 17th and 18th Centuries.

825. OCTAGON SCROLLED SKIRT PLAIN STRETCHER TABLE. 1690–1700.

826–828. HARPSICHORD AND CANE CHAIRS.

much satisfaction in a piece of furniture that may be left wholly as found. We discovered this piece in Plymouth in 1921.

Size: Top, 27¾ inches across. The frame is 21½ inches square. The hight is 26¼ inches and the table was probably not more than about half an inch higher originally.

Nos. 826–828. Large musical instruments of our period perhaps cannot be counted American. They were, as we suppose, imported, but their frames are American. We merely glance at the subject, and show two or three examples.

No. 826 is called a harpsichord. It is in the great room of the Benning Wentworth house at Newcastle, New Hampshire. One sees that the base is of a simple character. It is flanked by a good pair of chairs. The right-hand one has unusual and very interesting carving on the stretcher.

No. 829. A spinet which the author bought at Haddam, Connecticut, from the family in which it had been from time immemorial. The instrument was made in London by Jacobus Kirckman, about 1690. One should take note that the numbers on spinets have been mistaken for dates. The frame of this spinet is simple. The instrument was made to lift off from the base, and was not attached in any way. There were small spurs, like nails, filed to a point, on the frame, which so far engaged the body of the spinet when it rested upon the frame as to prevent its slipping. The shape of this instrument is quite like that of a small grand piano. It is light enough to be lifted and carried by one man. It is said that it belonged to the niece of David Brainard, a missionary to the Indians in Connecticut.

No. 830. An interesting spinet because of its extremely elongated Spanish feet, cut in very good pattern when their length is considered. This spinet, formerly in the author's collection, is, we believe, now the property of the Brookline Public Museum. It was made by Thomas Hitchcock. The date is about 1690. The wood is walnut with inlays in front.

The tops of these instruments were so thin that in many cases warping cannot be prevented in a modern house. The only method of overcoming this permanently is to make a series of very fine parallel cuts on the under side, and then to bring the top to the proper shape and glue it. The method of straightening curved woods by flame is very unsatisfactory. After a while the ancient warp will reassert itself. Old wood is like an old man — practically impossible to reform. We have seen so much useless effort put forth in the straightening of warped boards, that we are induced to make this remark.

SLATE TOP TABLES

STILL more rare than a chest-on-frame, and with less reason for existence, is the slate top table. The top consisted usually of an oblong surface of slate with chamfered corners, which was set flush into a frame of veneered walnut. The object of the slate top was to provide a surface for tea things, and so to save the disfigurement of a wood top. The veneered edge, however, was about five inches wide and was particularly susceptible to injury through wetting. The designers, therefore, of these tables placed their patrons in a worse plight than would have been the case had they never owned them.

It is said that the tops were made on the Continent, perhaps in Switzerland, or in Italy, and that the frames were made here. Very few examples, possibly a half dozen, are known in America. We presume that owing to their lack of appeal to common sense, and also owing to their extreme delicacy, few were made, and that when they were made they were not preserved for any length of time.

In one respect, however, we are quite thankful to the makers, because the style of these tables showed exquisite taste, and indicated that Americans in the seventeenth century knew what was what in the matter of elements of style. We cannot point to anything made since that period more charming, airy and dainty in outline.

No. 831 illustrates such a table, owned by the Antiquarian Society at Worcester. The turning is in the fashion of the gate-leg or of a very dainty tavern table of the period.

No. 832 is the top of the same table. It appears that a portion of the slate is new. The inlay is of an intricate and delicate pattern. Of course, we do not certainly know that the tops were not made here. There were cabinet makers capable of doing the work, since the method was similar to that in use on the walnut veneer highboys. The pattern, however, is more involved than that in use on highboys. This example has been shown in other works.

No. 833 is quite a different pattern of a slate-top table. The trumpet turning is especially delicate and fine. The feet, attached below the stretcher, which is a double lyre shape, are scrolled in bold curves and are doweled to the post through the stretcher. There was a finial at the intersection of the stretcher arms.

829. Spinnet Formerly Owned by Niece of David Brainard. 1690–1700.

830. Spinnet with Spanish Feet. 1690.

831. SLATE AND VENEER TOP TEA TABLE. 1690–1700.

832. THE TOP OF TABLE SHOWN ABOVE.

833. WALNUT TRUMPET TURNED X STRETCHER SCROLLED FOOT TEA TABLE.

834. SLATE AND VENEER TOP OF TABLE SHOWN ABOVE. 1690–1700.

835. Scalloped Skirt Tea Table. 1690–1700.

836. Slate and Veneer Top of Table Shown Above.

No. 834 is the top of the same table. The inlay is a very intricate and minute design, and has suffered through wetting, as we have indicated that it was likely to do.

The original slate entire is in place, although it is cracked. Below the slate there is a series of slats to rëenforce the back. The slate is so very thin that we presume the slats are original. Otherwise the top would have broken under slight pressure.

The wood is walnut, except, of course, the portions of the veneer, which are of other colors. This table is reputed to have been found near Boston, where it was bought, in 1923.

One notices at once the analogy between the turnings of these pieces and those of the six-legged highboy, and its lowboy to correspond. There is so little data on which to generalize that we cannot be certain where such a piece as this would be kept in a dwelling. In size, it is not very different from a lowboy. In the same room, the two pieces would complement one another and add very much to the charm.

Size: The top is $24\frac{5}{8}$ by $34\frac{7}{8}$ inches. The hight is $26\frac{5}{8}$ inches.

No. 835. This specimen of a slate top tea table is in better condition than the others.

Owner: Mr. Daniel Staniford of Boston.

Its turnings are similar to those in No. 831, but just a trifle heavier. We believe that in spite of the fact that we show two of these tables with gate-leg turnings, a greater number of them are found with the highboy turnings.

This specimen has a symmetrically scalloped valance under the drawer. The original handles assist us in forming conclusions as to the date.

The top has its original slate, which is far heavier than that in the last example described. The veneer in the design on this piece, however, is confined to one section of the top as seen. The veneer appears to be in apple wood. The stretchers are deeply and delightfully worn on three sides. The fourth side shows practically no wear. The grandfather of the owner of this table taught school, it is said, using the table for a desk.

Size: Top, 25 by 40 inches, the width of the board outside the slate being $5\frac{1}{4}$ inches. The frame is 25 by $19\frac{1}{2}$ inches. The hight is 28 inches.

Of course the rarity and the beauty of these tables make them desirable in the eyes of collectors.

LOWBOYS

THIS is another term for dressing tables. It is supposed to have arisen in jest, with a sly slur at the legs of these pieces and their corresponding pieces, the highboys. Lowboys are usually found in solid or in veneered walnut, when in the type of turning which corresponds with the earliest period of highboys. It was the time of the brass drop handle. The pieces are rather delicate and, as in the case of the highboy, they have for the most part been destroyed. Strangely enough, they are much more rare, and therefore more highly valued, than the highboys. It is very seldom nowadays that an example comes to light.

No. 837 is a lowboy with very curious and interesting turnings.

Owner: Mr. John H. Halford of Norristown, Pennsylvania.

We notice an extra member in the turning of the legs which is quite different from that in the usual lowboy, and follows no recognized type. It is quite as if a larger urn were superimposed upon a smaller one. It is characteristic that the feet should be large, as here. In fact, the diameter of the turning on the foot is as large as the largest section of the leg above.

We presume that this piece originally had drops on the spaces which correspond above to the positions of the legs on the six-leg pieces. Of course, the object of omitting the two extra legs on the lowboy was to allow the knees to go under the piece. For the same reason the X stretcher was employed. As in the case of the highboy, there is a lining of walnut about $\frac{1}{8}$ inch thick on the intrados of the arches, with an astragal molding on the outside. Of course, the object of this was to give a fine finish everywhere and to avoid the appearance of any end wood. The drawer scheme in this piece, a narrow drawer at the center and two deep drawers at the side, is the usual arrangement. One notices a cupid's bow or double ogee mold on the frame at the ends and an ogee arch in the center in front. This central arch was as a rule cut higher than the side arches, for the sake of leg room.

Nos. 838–843. The parlor of the Alden House at Duxbury. An important element of interest in this room is the flat arch over the fireplace. This is quite unusual, so much so that we have been guilty of stating that it never occurred. We have now found at least two examples, the other being in a house in Hanson. Of course the panel work was not

837. X Stretcher Walnut Lowboy. 1690–1700.

838–843. "John Alden House" Parlor, Duxbury.

844. Cross Stretcher Cup Turned Lowboy of Walnut. 1690–1700.

845. All Turned Stand. 1700.

846. Turned Stand. 1690–1710.

847. Bowl Turned Lowboy with Drops. 1690–1710.

848. Carved Foot Stove. Early 18th Century.

849. X Stretcher Trumpet Turned Lowboy. 1710–20.

850. Lacquered Cross Stretcher Table. 1690–1700.

original with the house, a bedroom of which we have already shown, and the date of which is supposed to be 1653. Panel work was added in dwellings of this sort beginning about 1720.

The pieces of furniture shown might have been in the house about 1720. The floor candle stand, with its inverted and weighted funnel base, is a type frequently found.

No. 844. A lowboy from which the drops on the front skirt are missing, but which has its finial at the intersection of the scrolled stretchers. The turning here corresponds with that of highboys of the inverted bowl or cup turning. The veneer is walnut with herringbone border. A single arch mold (astragal) was used a little earlier than the double arch mold. The bail handles with ornamental surfaces are of somewhat later date than the drop handles. This piece was bought not far from Boston. Certainly New England did possess a good number of lowboys.

Nos. 845–846. We insert here, for convenience, two stands, both of which are owned by Edward C. Wheeler, Jr. The turnings are dainty. That on the left has a drawer. We believe the top is too small. This stand is only 31 inches in hight. The piece on the right is of maple, in beautiful condition, and has plain stretchers. The top is oval and measures 17 by 23¾ inches, and the piece is 23½ inches high. The dates of both pieces range between 1690 and 1710.

No. 847 is a walnut cross-stretcher lowboy.

Owner: Mr. Edward C. Wheeler, Jr., of Boston. The huge middle drop is a striking feature and an amusing instance of how style dominated and pushed convenience to the wall in those days, as now. The basal scheme of a lowboy was to afford room as a dressing table. Of course one could not sit at such a table as this, and although we have named it a lowboy, we are more inclined to believe, since it has a single long drawer, and this peculiar conformation on the front, that it was merely a small table. This judgment does not at all detract from its importance. We shall later show another table of this type, certainly not designed as a lowboy. It will be seen that the larger drop is simply a reversed finial, a duplicate of that on the intersection of the unusually elaborate cross stretcher.

No. 848. A carved footstove, the top rosette being pierced for the sake of ventilation.

Origin: Pennsylvania.

Footstoves like this, carried in vehicles and taken into church, are still common enough because they are curious articles and, being small, they could easily be preserved. In this elaborate form, however, they are rare. We have seen another somewhat similar to this. It has a slide in one side to insert the tin container for the charcoal.

The top measures 9 by 8½ inches, and the hight is 7½ inches. It is of walnut. The date is uncertain, but probably in the eighteenth century.

No. 849. A trumpet-turned lowboy of walnut.

Owner: Mr. G. Winthrop Brown.

It has the double arch mold. The finials are interesting, being rather different from those we have seen. In fact, we hardly understand the motive. This is the first example in which the scroll stretcher has been at all simplified. The feet here are somewhat smaller than the other examples shown.

One should note that even in the walnut furniture the legs, especially in the highboys, are often of a lighter wood than walnut; basswood or poplar being often found. The turned section was sometimes painted, and naturally, being ornamental in its nature, it did not require the veneer which was applied to flat surfaces.

One sees here the thumb-nail molding, as is usual on the top of these pieces.

No. 850. A cross-stretcher table in maple. There is a label on the back of the drawer: "Table made 1700. Gilt 1847." The author was advised to remove the lacquer. The attempt, however, to do lacquer work in America at so late a period is thought to be sufficiently interesting to be allowed to remain, especially as it is rather successful.

We believe that the turnings are in pine. The drawer bottom is of pine. Obviously, this table was not made as a lowboy. It is much rarer than the lowboy. It forms, with the cross stretcher desk, stools, lowboy, slate top table, highboy and chair table, one of a large series of cross stretcher objects of sufficient number to furnish a room.

Size: Frame, 17¼ by 24½ inches. It is 28 inches high.

No. 851. A beautiful little lowboy of cherry.

Owner: Mr. Chauncey C. Nash.

This piece is one of the few of the period in cherry, with which we are acquainted, and it is the only lowboy we have encountered in the six-leg style. The turnings are odd and interesting. It was found in Stratham, New Hampshire, in the family with which it had always been. For a long time collectors declined to take it as the price was regarded as pro-hibitory. Any collector at the present time, however, would be only too glad to secure it. It was originally owned by Anna Rush, whose monument, erected by the women of Stratham, is in the cemetery.

The piece is all original, neither needing nor having had repairs.

Size: Top, 20½ by 34½ inches; hight, 30¼ inches. The frame is 17½ by 29½ inches.

One should take careful note of the shape of the scroll in the stretchers,

851. Unique Six Legged Lowboy of Cherry. 1710–20.

852. Tavern Table, Drop Leaf. 18th Century.

853. Unique Butterfly Table. 1690–1700.

854. Walnut Scrolled Skirt Table. 1710–30.

855. BUTTERFLY TABLE WITH DRAWER. 1700.

856. LARGE BUTTERFLY TABLE WITH PIERCED RING. 1700.

857.   Butterfly Table, Crane Bracket.   1700.

858.   Square Post Table.

859.   Trestle Foot Stand.

which is designed to follow the outlines of the skirt above.   This is the proper style, followed also on the end stretchers.

No. 852.   Placed here for convenience is an odd example of a light tavern table with a drop leaf, which, it is claimed, is original.   It is in the same wood and color as the top leaf and it is possible that it may be original.   Much discussion has arisen as to whether single, or in fact, any leaves ever appeared on tavern tables originally.   The author doubts their originality unless some of these tavern tables were made along toward the middle of the eighteenth century, as perhaps this example was.

BUTTERFLY TABLES

THIS class of tables, about which a good deal of sentiment seems to gather, is a curious instance of the fact that some little detail of construction may make a certain class of furniture very much sought for. While these tables are thought by some to have originated in Connecticut, they are found in sufficiently large numbers in eastern Massachusetts and southern New Hampshire to induce the author, at least, to believe that they should not be confined to Connecticut origin.

The name of course arises from the outline of the bracket which supports the leaf. In the earliest types we think the bracket was rather simple. These tables are found with both plain and turned stretchers, the turned stretcher being very rare. A characteristic of most examples is the rake of the legs one way. In this respect these tables are like many tavern tables. The collector, therefore, should be warned that it is a favorite trick of furniture forgers to place a butterfly top on the splayed leg frame of a small tavern table. One needs to be somewhat keen in the matter to avoid the fraud.

We may not have a better opportunity in this book to point out the rapid increase of spurious pieces of furniture in America. Twenty years ago the values of this furniture were so small that there was no inducement for the unscrupulous to forge the originals. With the present very high prices, however, there is a powerful stimulus in the underworld to supply the buyer with what he wants. Within the past two or three years we have encountered pieces sought to be passed off, which were constructed with the utmost skill, so as to rival the English imitations. We have in the past looked across the water for the masters of this depraved skill. A school, however, is being built up in this country that may soon rival its co-workers in the Old World.

We have long been accustomed to look askance, habitually, at furniture from the Continent, especially from Italy. We may now proceed with the greatest circumspection in relation to American pieces, especially if they are of the class now counted valuable.

One needs to have very much more acquaintance with old furniture than that possessed by the average collector, to detect a good counterfeit. It is one thing to be deceived ourselves and an even worse thing for a person to buy and present to a friend a counterfeit piece, under the supposition that it is real. Such an instance came to our attention.

860–861. BALL FOOT TABLE CUPBOARD, AND BUTTERFLY TABLE. 1700.

862. Butterfly Table, Original Top. 1700.

863. Drop Leaf Triangular Table.

864–867. Splayed Scrolled Table.

868. BUTTERFLY TABLE WITH DRAWER. 1700.

869. LIGHT BUTTERFLY TABLE. 1700.

870. BUTTERFLY TABLE WITH DRAWER. 1700.

871. VERTICAL LEG BUTTERFLY TABLE. 1700.

872. TRESTLE BUTTERFLY TABLE. 1690–1700.

873. STRONGLY FEATURED BURL BOWL.

874. Trestle Butterfly Table. 1690–1700.

875. Open Bracket Vertical Leg Butterfly Table. 1700.

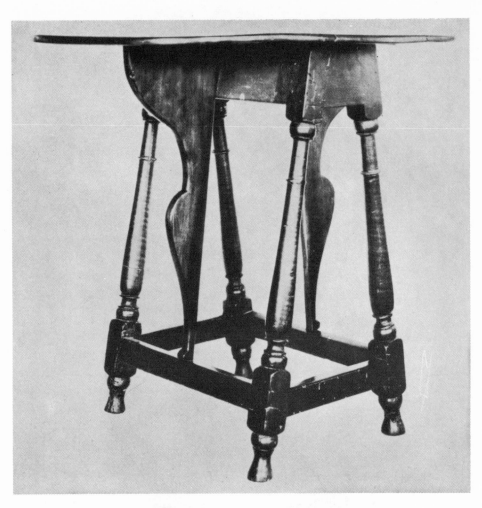

876. Butterfly Table without Drawer. 1700.

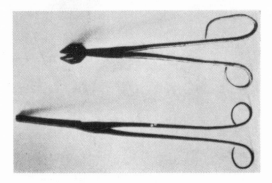

877–878. Curling Irons.

No. 853. A table supposed to be unique, and having elements that suggest the gate-leg.

Owner: Mr. H. W. Erving. The turnings, like the best gate-leg turnings, are carried out on the swivel framework used to sustain the leaves. There is a strut on a wedge shaped member which shuts into a slot in the frame, as shown. This piece is of the highest importance. It has been illustrated before. It suggests to us the style of the crane bracket, two examples of which will follow. It was, of course, necessary in this construction to make the bracket in the form of a T, cutting away the section that is to turn under the frame. The design is certainly of great interest, and quite successful.

Size: Of top, 33 by 37 inches.

No. 854. For convenience, we insert here a Pennsylvania tavern table, whose valance or skirt is cut in an odd series of curves, more attractive on the ends than on the front. Though the feet are lost, this table is an interesting specimen. One sees here the somewhat flat turnings, often characteristic in the legs of the Pennsylvania walnut tables, such as this is. It was in the author's former collection.

No. 855. A butterfly table with a good style of wing. One should here take note of the purpose of the raked leg, to form a wedge shaped frame. The wing or bracket which sustains the leaf is attached to the stretcher by the prolongation of the lower end, in the form of a dowel entering the stretcher. Above, in order to form a long bearing for the bracket on the leaf, the bracket is run past the frame up to the top, where, on the back edge, it engages with the fixed central board of the table with a dowel and bored hole similar to that below. Thus the bracket can be vertical, or nearly so, on the back. The turnings of this table are somewhat heavy, and may indicate an early period. The feet are partly worn away. One sees the overlapping drawer. The wood is maple, as usual.

No. 856. A large butterfly table, the property of the Rhode Island School of Design. It was in the author's former collection. It is the only example with which we have met having square leaves. We were never satisfied whether or not the top was original, but we have been assured that in this specimen it is. This table has an interesting detail in that there are sockets cut in the ends of the frame under the fixed portion of the top for the insertion of extended cleats to support an additional leaf. These sockets, however, are undoubtedly subsequent to the making of the piece. Thus a dining table of a good size was obtained. An interesting peculiarity of this piece is the cut out circle in the bracket, to give it a lighter effect, and some mark of ornament.

The wood is maple.

No. 857. A curly maple butterfly table with crane brackets.

Owner: The estate of Mrs. Reinholt Faelten of Boston.

The design of the brackets is admirable, though of course the effect of a butterfly wing is lost. Further, in construction there was a good deal of extra labor involved through the framing of the brackets.

Curly maple came into use, in some instances, before the close of the seventeenth century, we suppose. It is a beautiful material, and deserves much attention, such as it is receiving in these days. The principle of decoration is against the use of curly maple in a turning, as a turned piece of wood is decorative in itself and the double decoration at the same point is questionable taste, as well as being confusing to the eye. As a consequence, a curly grain in a turning, while frequently seen, cannot be counted as a point of merit. However, the makers as a rule avoided this curly grain because it was a very refractory material. Even on a plain surface it is impossible to smooth it except by grinding. Indeed, one of the charms of curly maple pieces is the ridgy effect apparent to the fingers when run over the surface.

Size: Top, 26½ by 35 inches; hight, 25½ inches.

No. 858. A stand whose square posts are chamfered. It came from the Churchill family, Newington, Connecticut. The top and drawer are of pine, and the top has gouge carving at the ends like that seen on many chests and boxes. It is the property of Mr. George Dudley Seymour, and is in the Wadsworth Atheneum.

Date: about 1700.

No. 859. An interesting little table owned by Mr. Chauncey C. Nash. One might almost call the shoe an instep foot. The openwork at the ends, cut in the form of a semicircle, is identical at the top and bottom. The material is pine. It would be fair to call this little piece a trestle table.

Date: about 1700.

Nos. 860–861. The former number is that of a small table cupboard with ball feet. It is the property, with the table on which it stands, of the Rhode Island School of Design. While we do not know the origin, we surmise it is from Pennsylvania.

The butterfly table below is small, and the curve of the brackets is plain.

No. 862. A maple butterfly table of good size. It has a drawer with knob and is all original, but lacks the balls on the feet. The tongued and grooved joint at the meeting of the leaf and the joint of this table is counted desirable as a mark of date, yet the date is not to be precisely fixed. We look for this joint, however, in furniture, before 1730.

879. TRESTLE TABLE WITH LEAVES. 1690–1710.

880–883. SNOW SHOES, SHOVEL, CHURN AND HOLLOWED BARREL.

884. ALL SPLAY LEGGED, SCROLLED SKIRT, DROP LEAF TABLE. 1690–1700.

885–886. TWO TURNED STANDS, PLAIN STRETCHERS. 1690–1720.

887. SMALL CROSS STRETCHER STAND. 1690–1700.

888–889. DARK LANTERNS.

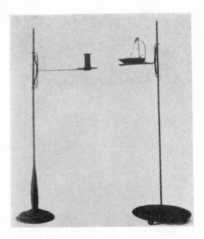

890–891. IRON FLOOR STANDS.

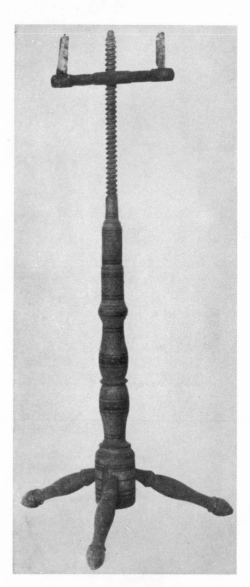

892. SCREW CANDLE STAND. 1690–1740.   893. SCREW STAND.

A feature of these tables, which we have not pointed out, could nevertheless be deduced. That is to say, the sides of the drawer slant inward to match the slant of the frame. Under the drawer there is often a thin rail or slant running lengthwise of the drawer to sustain it. The handles should always be small wooden knobs. When the table is very small there may not be room for a drawer.

Size: Top, 40½ by 45¾ inches. The width of the central board is 14½ inches. Hight, 25¾ inches, to which we suppose an inch and a half should be added for the lost feet.

No. 863. A table with a round top and three drop leaves and triangular frame. It is owned by the Metropolitan Museum.

A feature of much interest is that the top is set on a swivel and that, when it is swung, the three leaves, being relieved from their supports formed by the angles of the table, fall as soon as they have reached the sections made parallel with them by swinging. We have never seen another table of this character, though we have heard a report of one or two. In this instance, one notices two ball turnings at the feet, a rare thing. The posts here are vertical. In some of the previous examples they are raked. The date is about 1700.

Nos. 864–867. A square table with all legs raking. On two sides there is a scroll on the skirt. These tables are considered somewhat important and are not usual. Resting on the top are a noggin, a canteen, and a small tub.

No. 868. A butterfly table belonging to Mr. George Dudley Seymour. Curiously, the drawer seems never to have had a handle. One notices here a greater degree of elaboration in the contour of the butterfly wing. This specimen is of cherry. It is from the Captain Churchill House, Newington, Connecticut. It may have belonged to his forbears. The table is absolutely original, including its feet. The leaves are hung on large butterfly hinges. We should note, when we mention these hinges, that their name has nothing to do with their use in connection with a butterfly table. Mr. Seymour has a companion cherry butterfly table, also from the same house, which table has a rectangular top.

No. 869. A small butterfly table of good design, though simple.
Owner: Mr. H. W. Erving.
The long pear shaped feet correspond with the turning.

No. 870. A butterfly table from the collection of Mr. B. A. Behrend.
The wear of the stretchers is especially noticeable. The table is small with the usual oval top. The wood is maple.

No. 871. A butterfly table which varies from those we have shown in having a vertical frame. It was necessary therefore to change the construction of the wing, the upper part of which must engage with the under side of the frame, owing to the vertical construction. We have here, then, a wing suggestive of the first table shown under this heading.

No. 872. A combined butterfly and trestle-table. These are among the rarest of all American furniture specimens. The trestle foot is cut here in the form of a simple arc, and the stretcher is turned. The butterfly wings are not contoured, but are cut in a perfectly simple triangular form. It will be noted that on the upper part of these wings a portion of the triangle is cut away, and the part left is thinned to a bevel, so as to admit of the closing of the leaf. When the leaves are down, the table is only $7\frac{1}{2}$ inches across the top.

The source of the table is eastern Massachusetts, near Boston.

Size: The top is 31 by 26 inches. Hight, $23\frac{1}{2}$ inches. The spread of the trestle shoe is 14 inches. The square of the posts is $1\frac{3}{4}$ inches. It is $8\frac{1}{2}$ inches from the top of the stretcher to the floor. The width of the frame is $18\frac{3}{4}$ inches.

The hinges seem ancient, very. Nevertheless, the joint of the leaves is plain.

No. 873. A large, beautifully featured bowl of burl, one of fourteen in the collection of the author.

No. 874. A trestle and butterfly table.

Owner: Mr. Dwight Blaney.

The feet are somewhat more ornamental than in No. 872, and the butterfly wings have their usual curve. We do not at this date know of any other examples than these two, though there are many spurious pieces.

No. 875. A crane bracket table, a variant of the butterfly. One observes here the vertical frame. The turnings are all the same size. The crane bracket is framed. We have seen one or two other examples like this table. They are all painted black, as is this one, which was found in Westboro, Massachusetts.

It is from the author's former collection and is owned by Mr. Harry Long.

No. 876. A small butterfly table in curly maple.

Owner: The estate of George F. Ives.

The top is very narrow, being only 6 inches outside the frame, leaving no room for a drawer. The top is $23\frac{1}{2}$ by 33 inches. The frame at the base is 14 inches wide at the ends, showing a rapid spread.

We should call attention to the fact that in all the butterfly tables the wings are thin, varying from $\frac{1}{2}$ inch to $\frac{3}{4}$ inch. We have seen some restorations made with thicker boards for the wings.

Nos. 877–878. A curling iron and love-lock iron.

Owner: Mrs. De Witt Howe.

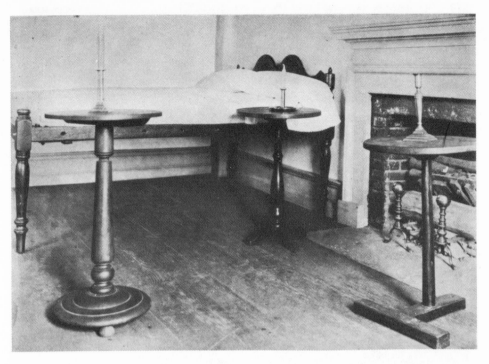

894–897. Candle Stands and "Hired Man's" Bed. 18th Century.

898–899. X Base Candle Stands. 1690–1730.

900–906. PINE SETTLE, CARVER CHAIRS, ROASTING JACK, CANDLE BOX.

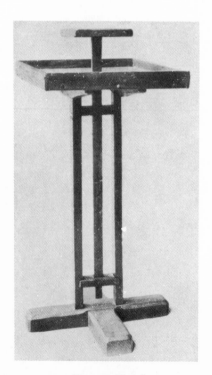

907. DOUBLE TOP STAND.

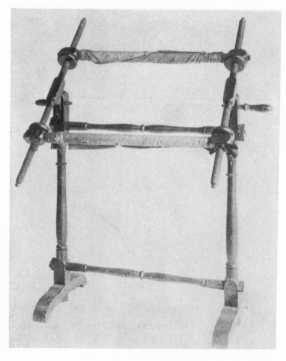

908. EMBROIDERY FRAME.

909–910. Spoon Rack and Stand.   911–913. Pipe Box, Stand, etc.

914. Six Branch Chandelier with Wood Hub. 18th Century.

915–916. Cross Base Stands. 18th Century.

917. Chandelier with Globe Center. 18th Century.

No. 879. A very rare table of which we have seen only one other example. It is built in the trestle pattern, but has leaves, which are held in place by a double-ended tongue, swiveled at the center and holding up both leaves. The type is most interesting and important.

Owner: Mrs. De Witt Howe.

Nos. 880–883. The snowshoes on the left have leather leggings attached. We may presume that the owner devised this scheme because he could not remember, like some other boys of a subsequent generation, where he had left his belongings. The shovel is all quartered oak in one piece, and is very sturdy as we can testify, it having served in the case of a recent great storm.

The churn was presented to the author by Mr. Stephen Alden of Brockton, and it came down in the Alden family. The barrel at the right is hollowed out of a single log, and has a bottom board nailed in. These barrels were sometimes of hornbeam. We suppose this one to be in maple.

No. 884. An unusual drop leaf table in which all legs rake, and with a scrolled skirt on the side. The wood is maple. This table is difficult to classify, and we have therefore placed it in this position. It is somewhat larger than a tavern table, and somewhat smaller than a dining table. The feet are missing.

It was in the former collection of the author.

Size: 44 by 52 inches, the long dimension in this case being with the grain, as the leaves are narrow.

Nos. 885–886. Two stands of similar but not identical turning.

They are the property of Mr. Edward C. Wheeler, Jr.

That on the left has an oval top. The hight, as it stands, is $21\frac{3}{4}$ inches, but it, as well as its companion, has lost the feet. The top is 20 by 31 inches. The table on the right one might say was a joint stool, so far as the size is concerned. It is 19 inches high and the legs slant or rake one way, as is usual in a joint stool. The rectangular top is 12 by 18 inches.

No. 887 is a very rare little stand, the photograph of which was furnished the author by Mr. Henry V. Weil. A feature of special attraction, of course, is the turned cross stretchers combined with the raked legs.

Nos. 888–889. Two little dark lanterns belonging to Mr. H. W. Erving. They are of much interest, though we suppose the date to be at least as late as the eighteenth century.

Nos. 890–891. Two candle stands with cast discs for bases, and with plain rods for standards. One of these has a bracket, for the lamp, in the toggle joint or folding pattern. The other stand is shaped to receive a Betty lamp. The origin is Pennsylvania, and the date unknown. It is probably somewhat late, and may be the nineteenth century.

CANDLE STANDS

W E HAVE previously, for convenience's sake, in the arrangement of the volume, inserted a number of light stands or candle stands of wood or iron. We wish now to discuss separately a number of these pieces which of late have come to occupy no small share of the collector's attention. They are found perhaps more often than otherwise with tripod bases. Sometimes, however, there is a heavy, clumsy block as a base, and sometimes there are four legs. Again there is a turned disc for a base. The greater part of these stands which we shall now show are adjustable for hight.

No. 892. This is one of two maple stands of this character found. The characteristics are a disc in the shape of a threaded washer on a wooden screw, to afford a small work table or a rest for implements. Above it is a cross member sustaining a candle at each end. The disc table has a slight raised edge like a tray. A peculiar feature of merit is the pair of wood screws below the candles. The object was to force the candle up as it burned. It is a touch giving completion to the piece and greatly enhancing its importance. The turning of the cross bar is very good. The hub, as we may call it, into which the post enters, has three wide straddling feet of simple turning. The main post finishes in a simple handle or finial. The candles are kept in place by tin candlesticks slit at the bottom so as to be attached to the crossbar.

Origin: Concord, New Hampshire. The condition is perfect. The surface is in the original natural color of old maple, a very pale yellow.

No. 893. A candle stand in the George F. Ives Collection.

The collector is warned that among all the spurious pieces of furniture now found, probably there is no subject oftener counterfeited than the candle stand. The author saw no fewer than a dozen, all absolutely of recent manufacture, in one shop, at one time. They might easily deceive a novice. They have also been so well done as to deceive experienced collectors. It is a favorite method to take the legs of Pennsylvania spinning wheels and insert them in the re-turned posts of old beds.

Nos. 894–897. A series of candle stands in the Nathan Hale mansion at Coventry, Connecticut. Mr. George Dudley Seymour is the owner. The stand on the left is a good example of its kind, being all turned. The diameter of the top is $16\frac{1}{4}$ inches, and the hight is 28 inches.

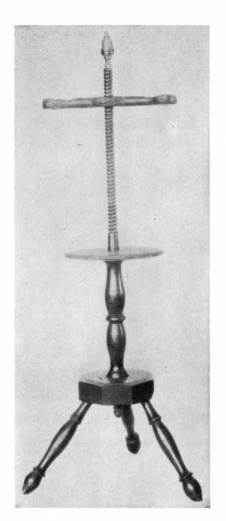

918–920. Tripod Screw Stands. 18th Century.

921–929. Coffee Grinder, Lamps, Nursing Bottle, Etc. 18th Century.

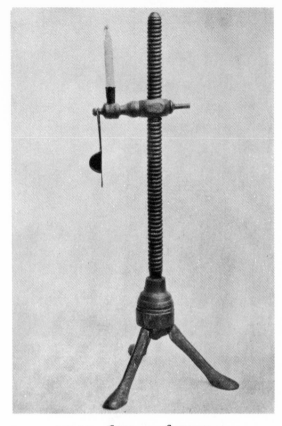

930. SCREW STAND.

931–932. STAND AND SNUFFERS.

933. PIERCED TIN LANTERN.

934. SMOKE JACK. 1760.

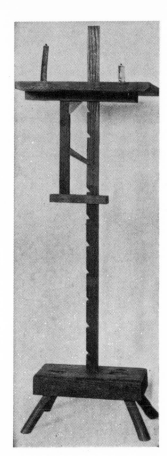

935–936. Tripod and Ratchet Stands. 18th Century.

937. Hard Pine Triangular Table.

938. Triangular Table.

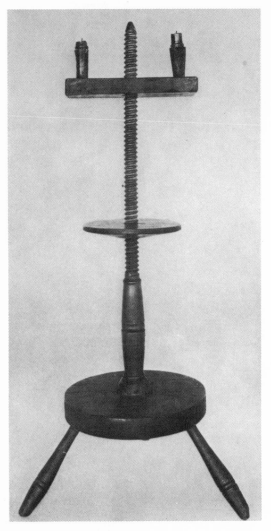

939. Tripod Screw Stand.

940. Pod Stand.

941–945. Noggin, Lamps, Sconce, Etc.

The remote stand by the side of the bed has a cross base, arched, and supporting a maple shaft, mortised to receive a profiled cleat sustaining the round pine top. It is 16 inches in diameter and 27 inches high. To the right is a T base stand, so made that the part supporting the shaft is between the feet of the user who places his feet on the cross stretcher. The post is maple. The bed is of oak, an unusual material.

The diameter at the top is 17¼ inches and the hight is 25 inches. It is presumed that these stands are of the eighteenth century.

No. 898. A stand from Henry V. Weil. It is made so that it is difficult to overturn. One notices the notches carved on three sides of the stubbed feet. The top is octagonal.

No. 899. A stand with a massive post, chamfered, with stops. It will be noted that the ends of the cross members are notch carved. It is almost impossible to date these pieces, but they may be late seventeenth or early eighteenth century.

Nos. 900–906. A room showing seventeenth and eighteenth century furniture. In the distance, against the plaster on the left, there is a tall iron candle stand. Over the fireplace hangs a bar on iron hooks. It was used to air ironed articles; sometimes a checkered apron, perhaps, was allowed to hang there as sort of momentous warning to the youngsters.

On the right is a pine stool which is of a later period. Over the head of the grandfather, against the wall, there is a tin cylindrical candle box. The feet of the young lady are on a braided rug all made of corn husks, said to have been used in this form by the Indians. We doubt, however, whether the knowledge of braiding and rug making came to our ancestors from that source. No doubt some of their basket work was learned from the Indians.

One sees in this picture the huge proportions of a summer beam, the great beam overhead at the left sustaining the floor timbers. The room is the kitchen of the Iron Works House, Saugus.

No. 907. A very rare, possibly unique, candle stand belonging to Mrs. J. Insley Blair. The shaft or movable post at the center is guided by a crossbar with slots at the ends. When the shaft is elevated it can be fixed at any position by a small pin inserted in one of the holes at the elevation of the fixed mortised member near the top, through which the shaft runs. On the top of the shaft is a small square platform for the candle. The larger table top has a rim about it.

No. 908. An embroidery frame. A very neatly shaped arched trestle foot supports it. The cross arms above are made as screws on which the large wooden nuts turn to make the work taut. A pair of end screws on the posts are also used to give the work the proper slant.

Owner: Mr. Edward C. Wheeler, Jr.

The date may be the eighteenth century.

No. 909.   A square base stand in which the cross members are gently rounded to the floor.   On the stand is set a very excellent spoon rack with simple carvings between the racks and a tree decoration above, at the top of all being a knob.   These pieces probably originated among the Knickerbocker inhabitants of the banks of the Hudson, where several others have been found.

Owner: Mr. B. A. Behrend.

Nos. 911–913.   A boldly-turned stand with turned tripod feet.   On the stand is a pipe box with pierced heart ornaments, and a drawer for the tobacco.   On the right, with an iron standard and a bowl below it, is an adjustable Betty lamp.   They are owned by Mr. G. Winthrop Brown.

No. 914.   A chandelier of wood and strips of tin terminating with scalloped saucers of tin, in which the candle is placed.   The style is excellent and such articles are rare.

Owner: The estate of George F. Ives.

Nos. 915–916.   Two similar candle stands; that on the left, though more ornate, is perhaps not so good as that on the right, massiveness in these old stands being a point of merit.   Both stands are shaped with raised bases terminating in bracket feet.   The right hand stand has a chamfered shaft with stops.   They belong to the eighteenth century.

No. 917.   A tin chandelier in the George F. Ives Collection.   At the center of the tin hoop from which the arms extend is set a large globe, and the sustaining chains are sufficiently obvious.

No. 918.   A tripod candle stand, the hub of which is decorated with scratch carving.   The table is set on a turned base and, while movable, is not adjustable for hight, as is the crossbar above it.

Nos. 919–920.   Candle stands, the lower one of which has a rim and the upper one of which is designed to be set on a table, being small and therefore very unusual.   These three pieces belong to the George F. Ives Collection.

Nos. 921–929.   Household utensils of hardware belonging to Mr. Francis Mireau, Fountain Inn, Doylestown, Pennsylvania.   The large piece above in the shape of a boat is sharply slanted toward the center, where the sides meet at an angle.   The disc with handles was rolled back and forth and coffee was thus ground.   The piece is cast.   The heart-shaped flat iron speaks for itself, and so does the miniature fluid lamp.   On the left below is a quaint padlock.   The next on the right is a vessel of tin with a handle and a snout which served as a nipple for a nursing bottle.   The tube extends to the bottom of the vessel, so that the infant could

946–947.   Two X Base Stands.   1690–1730.

948–951.   Four Candle Stands.   18th Century.

952–955. CANDLE STANDS AND SCRAPER CANDLE. 18th CENTURY.

956–958. TRESTLE STAND AND ADJUSTABLE STAND.

959–961. THREE LANTERNS. 18th CENTURY.

962. LARGE SHIP LANTERN.

963. GLASS REFLECTOR LANTERN.

964–970. Bed Room with Odd Chest and Early Rocking Chair, etc.

971. Camp Meeting Lamp.

972. Carved Spoon Rack.

get the last drop. It is a most interesting little piece, but not half so much so as another which we have seen, with a nozzle going out from either side; and which was obviously intended to feed twins!

The next articles are pretty well known, being probably the earliest forms of candle molds, before their time candles being dipped. On the right is an ink well.

No. 930 is a quaint candle stand with crudely shaped feet, something in the form of a hoof.

Nos. 931–932. This candle stand belongs to Mr. J. Stodgell Stokes. It is most quaint in the shaping of the feet, and their attachment to the hub. It is very unusual, in being provided with only one candle instead of one at either end of a crossbar as usual. There depends from the end of the knob on the candle holder a pair of wrought iron snuffers.

No. 933. A large lantern now named for Paul Revere who, we doubt not, would have repudiated it. Such lanterns were used in the nineteenth century and perhaps in the eighteenth.

No. 934. A smoke jack which the author took out of the kitchen chimney in the Wentworth Gardner house in Portsmouth, repaired, photographed, and returned to its place. It fitted into the flue of the chimney so that the draft revolved the mechanism with its worm gear. The shaft protruded through the face of the chimney, and to the end of it was attached the small chain belt that turned the jack. A most interesting and fascinating contrivance, and extremely rare, if not unique, in this country.

No. 935. A simple candle stand with legs almost like sticks.

No. 936. A ratchet stand with four stick legs. The piece is odd in that the whole mechanism to which the pawl is attached rises and falls with the crossbar.

Owner: The George F. Ives Collection.

The date of these pieces may be the eighteenth century.

No. 937. A three-cornered table of yellow pine. It is very heavy, exceeding the weight of most oak pieces. It was purchased in New York, but is probably derived from a point somewhat farther southwest.

No. 938. A three-cornered rake legged table belonging to Mr. Frederick K. Gaston of New York. It is a most interesting piece. It follows the lines of the earliest Windsor turnings, so much so that one of its legs might be compared, except for length, with a Pennsylvania blunt arrow turned chair leg. One notices that the round stretchers are placed at different elevations in order not to weaken the wood. The posts at the top are run into a block on which the beveled circular table is fixed.

Size: Diameter of the top, 14¼ inches. Total hight, 22½ inches.

No. 939.   A stand in which the hub and the miniature table seem to be turned but are really worked out on a bench.   The legs and the post, otherwise called the shaft, are turned.   The crossbar is decorated by gouge turnings.   The piece is attractive, partly owing to the size of the table, which is only 6¾ inches in diameter.

The hight is 31½ inches.

No. 940.   A ratchet candle stand with pods or sockets of wood into which the candle was dropped.   A small block within this socket is moved up and down by a little metal clip extending through a slot in the side, and thus enabling one to regulate the hight of the candle.   The base is formed of a slab through which the posts are mortised.   It is the quaintest of all stands so far known to the author.

Nos. 941–945.   A series of articles in the George F. Ives Collection. The second is a magnifying lamp.   The sconce with three candlesticks is very good.   Next we have a swivel, otherwise called a ship lamp, which can be carried or hung on the wall; and last is a tinder box.

No. 946.   An excellently done stand with an especially good base, not so much for its artistic properties as for its sense of stability and quaintness.   The heavily turned post is good.

No. 947.   This is the best stand we have seen, in design.   The piece is walnut.   The shaft, which is fluted, is set on at a diagonal.   The feet are well molded.   The base was arched at one time more markedly than now, before perhaps an inch of wear occurred.   The left hand piece is 26½ inches high and 12 inches in diameter.   The right hand piece is 25½ inches high and 12 inches in diameter.

They date from the earlier part of the eighteenth century.

Nos. 948–951.   Four stands of various outlines.   That on the left resembles one we have shown in having a T head, on one member of which, the chamfered post, stands.   They are from the collection of Mr. B. A. Behrend, and are of various dates, probably all of the eighteenth century.

No. 952.   A candle stand with an arched cross base and an adjustable crossbar.

Owner: Mr. Hollis French.

No. 953.   An adjustable stand of odd construction.   The lower part of the base is hollow, and the smaller post rises and falls within the base.

Owner: Mr. B. A. Behrend.

No. 954.   A candle stand with a stick leg base, and a candle-stick which is hooked upon a bar.   The bars afford a range of elevation.

Owner: Mr. B. A. Behrend.

The three last described are of the eighteenth century.

973. Wool-Spinning Wheel. 17th and 18th Centuries.

974. Hutch Table.

975. Flax Wheel. 18th Century.

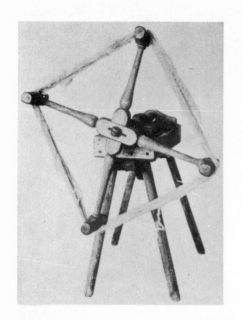

976–979. YARN REELS. 18th CENTURY.

980–983. Great Room of Ipswich Historical Society, Yarn Reel, etc.

984. Raked, Scrolled Table. 1690–1710.

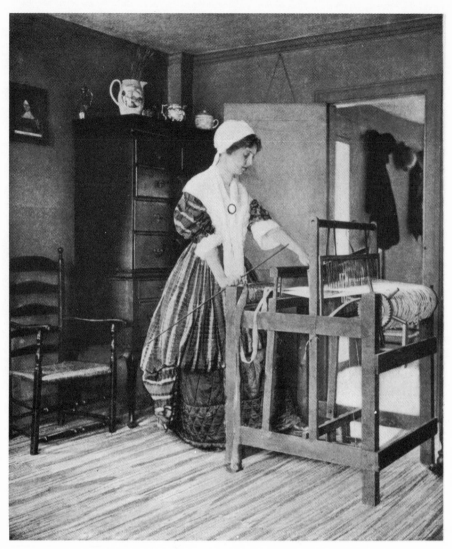

985. A Rag Rug Loom. 17th and 18th Centuries.

986–989. Burl Bowls, Mortar and Toddy Stick. 18th Century.

Nos. 956–957.   A small trestle stand similar to two others which we have shown.   It is a rare piece.   The lantern is of a late type.

Owner: Mr. B. A. Behrend.

Date: 1660–1690.

No. 958.   A rarely odd candle stand the feet of which are merely stubs inserted in bored holes.   The shaft is adjustable for hight, by a screw in the base.   The photograph is furnished by Mr. Henry V. Weil, who owned the piece.

Date: 1700–1750.

Nos. 959–961.   In these lanterns we have various types of the eighteenth or early nineteenth century.   One or two of them are rarely good.

Nos. 962–963.   Two heavy and quaint lanterns which perhaps do not require description.

Nos. 964–970.   A late seventeenth century room arranged as a bedroom.   The bed is of oak and the chest on the left is one which we have not illustrated although we have shown one similar to it.   The portrait belongs to the early nineteenth century.   The walls are properly done for the simple period of the eighteenth or the finer period of the seventeenth century.   The rocking chair on the right is one of several discovered within a few years, having an enlarged post at the bottom bifurcated for rockers.   We think that the bed has been cut down from a high-poster.   It must have been a wonderful specimen in its day.

The chair against the wall in the background over the table has a slat back and square posts.   We do not otherwise feature it, as its American origin is questioned.

No. 971.   A camp-meeting lamp throwing light to every quarter, and not two-faced, but four.   It is of tin.

No. 972.   A spoon rack and knife box.   It is carved in the Friesian design on the front and ends of the box, and with checker work in the back, and above with a pine tree.   Its condition is wholly original.

No. 973.   A spinning wheel for wool shown in operation.   Such wheels are not rare and occupy a good deal of room.   The garret is the place for them.   Those who spun for hours used a spoke stick or wheel stick to whirl the wheel and avoid blistering the fingers.   A good spinner would do perhaps six hundred yards of linen in a day, but we are not aware how much the wool wheel, deftly handled, would produce.

No. 974.   An amusing little hutch table which is sketched here rather than photographed.   The top swings so that the piece could be put against the wall.   The cubby under the top was thus open.

No. 975.   The usual type of the spinning jenny on which linen thread was made, the distaff being of especially good construction with turned ends connected by bowed ribs.

Nos. 976–979. Four forms of reels, all of them having some method to warn the user by a click when a skein had been wound, so that count might be kept, or the skein cut off at that point.

No. 977. This is adjustable on its shaft for winding hanks of the different lengths, for what purpose we do not know.

Nos. 980–983. The great room of the Saltonstall House, used by the Historical Society of Ipswich, Massachusetts. It has been called, by those competent to judge, the best seventeenth century room in America. It has the crossed summer beam which has sprung from the great weight attached so as, in the center, to hit the head of a man of average hight. Those who study such matters tell us that the stature of man has increased since the seventeenth century. The cross summer beam was a poor method of construction, as the mortise on the huge cross timber weakened the main beam. The beautiful quarter round chamfer of the main beam, with its good chamfer stop, here appears quite plainly.

On the right, attached to a table edge, is a collapsible reel such as was used in the nineteenth century. It was very convenient. We do not elsewhere show a tin oven or jack. They did not come in until the quainter, heavier early type, resting on the andirons, went out. Neither do we at all like them, as when they are used, they cumber a room and prevent a view of the fire. They are removed after use. They belong to the last part of the eighteenth century.

No. 984. A stand with odd turnings. It is meritorious from the shaped bracket, which is, of course, cut on the skirt of the frame. It rakes on every side.

Owner: The George F. Ives Collection.

Size: Top, 24 by 31 inches. It is 27 inches high. It probably belongs late in the eighteenth century.

No. 985. To carry through illustrations of most of the occupations of the early days, we illustrate a rag carpet loom in operation. The lady wears one of the quilted petticoats, which she is ambitious to have us know she possesses. She is weaving the sort of carpet on which she stands. The house is that formerly owned by " Ole Bill Spear " in North Pembroke.

Nos. 986–989. Bowls of burl and a mortar of the same. To collectors who are just beginning, a mortar has some fascination, but unless it has some special features, as in this case, it is of little value. The stick lying on the table, and with a bulbous end, is to crush sugar and, undoubtedly, was sometimes used for making toddy.

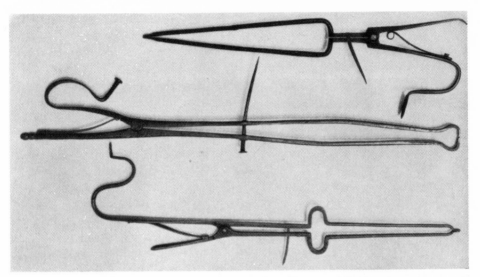

990–992. Three Fine Types of Pipe Tongs. 18th Century.

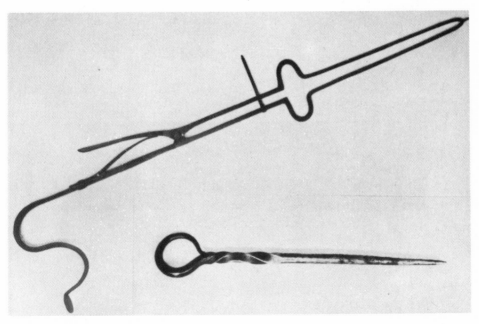

993–994. Fine Pipe Tongs and Ornamental Skewer. 18th Century.

995. STUMP FRAME LOOKING GLASS. 17th CENTURY.

996. LOOKING GLASS WITH INLAY. 1710–20.

997. LOOKING GLASS, FRAME WITH MOLDED LINING. 1690–1700.

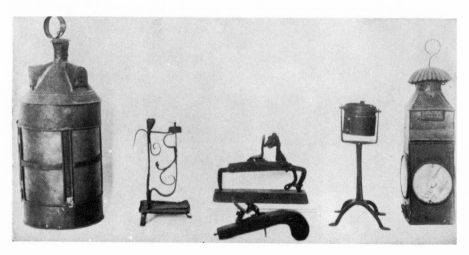

998–1002. HORN LANTERN, SPARKERS, ETC. 18th CENTURY.

1003–1004. QUILL WORK SCONCES. 1720.

1005. PETIT POINT NEEDLEWORK PICTURE. 17th CENTURY.

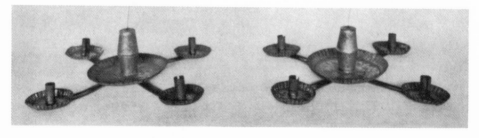

1006–1007. A PAIR OF TIN CHANDELIERS. 18th CENTURY.

1008. A Quill Work Double Sconce. 1710–20.

1009. LOOKING GLASS FRAME. 1700–20.

1010. LOOKING GLASS AND FRAME.

1011. LOOKING GLASS. 1700–10.

Nos. 990–992. Three remarkably good pipe tongs belonging to Mr. Henry Ford. The pair at the top is quite like one in the author's collection, and in that of Mr. Erving. The piece at the bottom was slightly repaired in its thumb-piece. It is otherwise original, and of very delicate contour. The central piece is most quaint. We have never seen anything else like it.

Nos. 993–994. No. 993 is so nearly like the one illustrated above that only by taking the articles in one's hand can the slight differences be seen. It is at the Wayside Inn, South Sudbury, and belongs to Mr. Henry Ford.

No. 994 is a decorated ceremonial skewer with reversed spiral. It was intended, no doubt, to withdraw the ordinary skewer on the top of the roast in the kitchen, and to insert this skewer when the meat went onto the table. It thus served not only to hold the roast together, but could be used to steady it in carving. It was presented to the author by Mr. Chetwood Smith, and was found in the attic of the General Eliot house in Sutton. General Eliot was a Revolutionary officer, and no doubt used this skewer.

LOOKING–GLASSES

IT HAS not yet been possible to ascertain definitely the origin of the finer looking-glass frames found in America before 1720. This remark applies particularly to the veneered walnut frames which were used during that period. We have every reason to suppose, however, that many of the frames were imported. At the same time, we believe it probable that some of them were made in this country.

Regarding the glass, which was as a rule, and perhaps always, plate, with a very soft bevel, scarcely observable in some lights, we know that that was invariably made abroad in our period.

In showing a few looking-glasses, therefore, it should be carefully understood that the only claim made for them is that they have been in America a great while. This remark would not apply to the obviously American simple small pine frame made in imitation of the finer walnut frames.

No. 995. A bead work frame in yellows, tans, greens and blues. The initials M. B. and the date 1660 are wrought in among the beads. The flower forms seem not to be emblematic, though the conventionalized rose may be so regarded. The flower in the lower right hand corner is unmistakably an iris.

This frame has its original beveled plate glass. In order to exclude objectionable reflections, it is covered in this picture.

Owner: Mr. L. G. Myers.

The so-called stump frame is the earliest of which we have any examples in America. They are very rare indeed.

No. 996. A looking-glass of satinwood with a walnut outside edge. The top has three inset panels of corresponding design. Originally the inlay covered the entire top. The veneer between the panels is now missing.

Size: The frame measures 3 inches across the molding. It is inlaid with Thuya and tulip wood. Size of glass, $13\frac{1}{4}$ by $16\frac{3}{4}$ inches.

Owner: Mr. Francis Hill Bigelow.

No. 997. A heavy looking-glass with its original glass, from which, however, the silvering has been cleaned off. The glass is now used to cover a coat-of-arms. The frame is beautifully decorated with marquetry of the period of 1700. This glass was sold from the Wayside

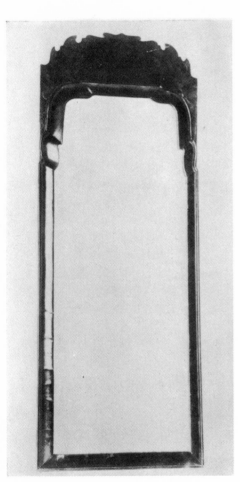

1012. LOOKING GLASS. 1710–20.   1013. LOOKING GLASS. 1710–20.

1014–1015. LOOKING GLASSES. 1710–20.

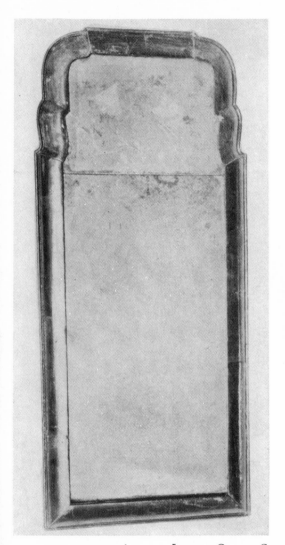

1016–1017. Looking Glasses, Cut Glass and Painted Tops. 1710.

1019. SCONCE GLASS. 1700–30.

1020. LOOKING GLASS. 1700–10.

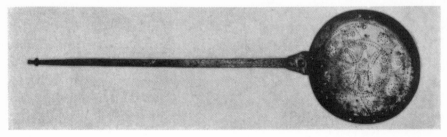

1021. WARMING PAN WITH DECORATED BRASS LID, IRON HANDLE. 18th CENTURY.

1022. LOOKING GLASS. 1700–20.   1023. GLASS, CUT TOP. 1710–20.

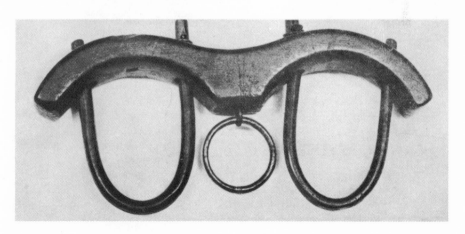

1024. DOUBLE GOOSE YOKE.

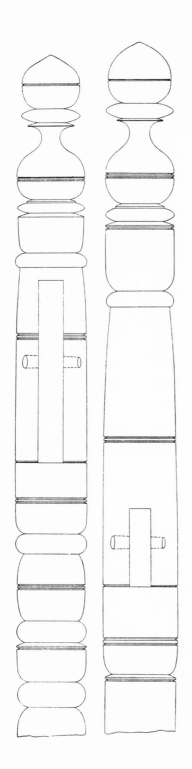

1027. SPINNING JENNY.

1025–1026. 17th CENTURY BED POSTS.

1028. CUPBOARD LATCH.

Inn, Sudbury, at the auction of its contents some fifty years ago.   It had been painted so that when it was sold, its character as a walnut and inlaid frame was not suspected.   The cresting is missing, but the condition of the frame is otherwise quite perfect.

Owner: Mr. George W. Hunt of South Sudbury, who inherited the glass from his father, who in turn purchased it at the auction.   The arms are those of the family who for many generations conducted the Inn, but are a copy.

Nos. 998–1002.   The first object is a horn lantern.   The author has one quite like it.   The name lantern, formerly lanthorn, has no reference to the horn of which its transparent substance was composed.   The word is not of English derivation.   The object, of course, in using the horn was to secure a material at once transparent and unbreakable.   We do not know when glass was first used in lanterns, but we should probably not date an example like this earlier than the beginning of the eighteenth century.

The next three objects may or may not be American, but the presumption is strong against the scrolled candle stick, which has to us an Irish suggestion.   The fire-makers or sparkers were no doubt made in the simple forms here.   The more elaborate forms are usually foreign. The fat lamp is discussed elsewhere.   The lantern at the right is an interesting, but not an early, type.

Owner: The George F. Ives Collection.

Nos. 1003–1004.   A remarkable pair of quill work sconces.   The frames are in all respects similar in styles and material to looking-glass frames of the period.   The obvious reason is that the looking-glasses themselves were often used as sconces.   The designer of these sconces fitted his frames with decorative materials designed to catch the light in front. The frames are of walnut.   The vase design, with rosettes and border, is of paper gilded on the edge.   The flowers, principally carnations and tulips, are made of wax which is perhaps mixed with mica.   Each petal is edged with silver wire.   The colors are red, blue, purple and white, of varying shades.   The whole sparkles from the light of the candle below.

They were made by Ruth Read, daughter of the Hon. John Read, a lawyer of distinction in Boston between 1722 and 1749.

In "Gold and Silver of Windsor Castle," 1911 (p. XXXI), Mr. E. Alfred Jones refers to this pair of simple scrolled candle brackets as being typical of such in use in England during the reign of Queen Anne. None of the English specimens seem to have survived the melting-pot. Similar brackets may be observed in Hogarth's engravings, "The Laughing Audience " and " The Analysis of Beauty." This pair of brackets was made by Knight Leverett of Boston (1703–53), and is engraved R R 1720.

We distinguish here between the sconce brackets which hold the candles, and the sconce, which is the portion against the wall — the framed section.

The pieces are supposedly unique. Their effect is excellent.

In not a few instances glasses probably had sconce brackets which have been lost, the sockets even being removed, so that there is scarcely a trace of their former location. The effect of looking-glasses with candles was not overlooked by the designers of the period. The fashion of using such candles was continued into Chippendale's time and even later, only in the later time the candles were placed at one side rather than below the glass. We may suppose that the fashion of cutting the surface of the glass in ornamental forms was a persistence of the decorative idea such as appears in the pair of sconces before us.

Owner: Mr. Francis Hill Bigelow.

Size of each: 9 by 21 inches.

The frames are veneered, apparently in walnut, $\frac{3}{4}$ inch wide, and are now painted black.

No. 1005. A framed petit point needle work picture of the seventeenth century. With its rich coloring, quaint drawing and perspective, it is characteristic of the period, and is of particular interest owing to the fidelity of the costumes displayed. It is introduced here, however, on account of the frame, which is of pine, well molded and with a wide gold line. In order to show the cloud effect, the top is made with a double arch, and should be compared with sconce No. 1008.

Owner: Mr. H. W. Erving.

Origin: Probably American.

Nos. 1006–1007. A pair of tin chandeliers. They were bought in New Haven. They were the first instance we have come upon of a pair. One notices that the word chandelier is derived from the old spelling for candle. Compare chandler, a dealer in candles. These pieces are in their original condition. The measurement across the arms is 21 inches. The middle disc is $8\frac{1}{4}$ inches in diameter, and the saucer bases of the individual candles are 4 inches in diameter. All edges are crimped. They are suspended by a wire.

No. 1008. A sconce in quill work. One sees at the bottom the bases upon which the arms of the candles are attached. This piece, together with No. 1003, is the only one of the sort known. They were of much importance and involved a vast degree of labor. One sees in this

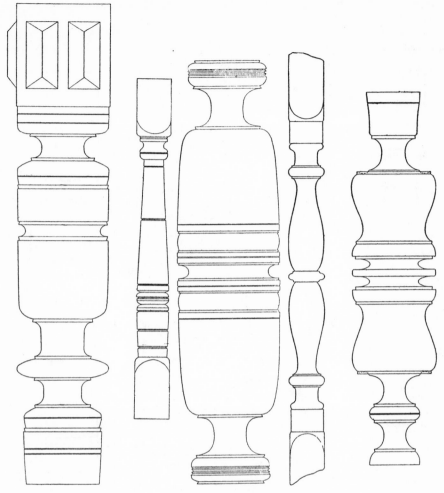

1029–1033. COURT CUPBOARD POSTS. 1640–1700.

example an arrangement of flower and leaf design with birds in the foliage.

Owner: Mr. Francis Hill Bigelow.

No. 1009. A decorated looking-glass. The frame is small and is painted in scrolls, which do not show at all clearly. The frame is said to have belonged to Peregrine White, though we do not know what the evidence is. It will be remembered that he was born on the Mayflower in Provincetown Harbor, and that we are supposed to have his cradle at Pilgrim Hall, Plymouth. He lived to a great age. Many articles have come down to us from him. He was the only original member of the Pilgrim band who lived into the eighteenth century. We believe this looking-glass to be American.

[*Continued on page 635.*]

1034–1037. 17th CENTURY TABLE LEGS.

1038–1042. 17th CENTURY TABLE LEGS.

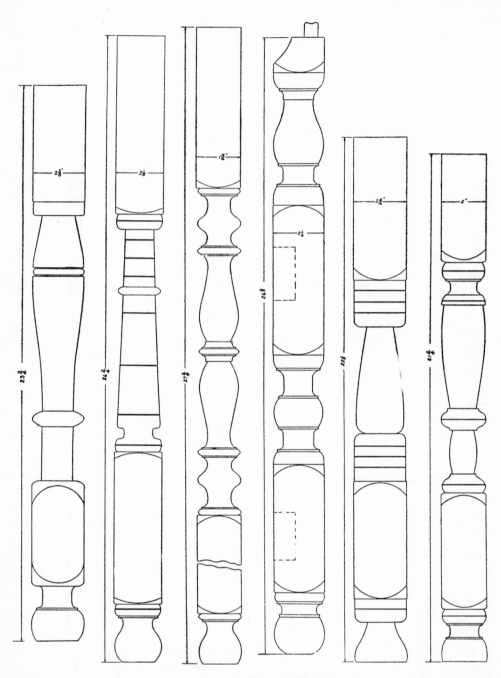

1043–1048.   17th Century Table Legs.

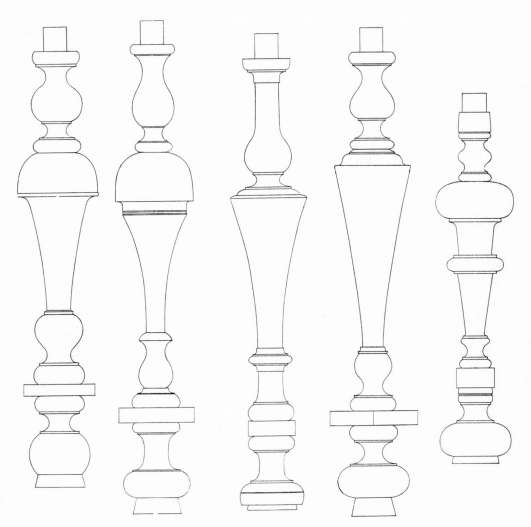

1049–1053. Highboy and Lowboy Legs, 1690–1720.

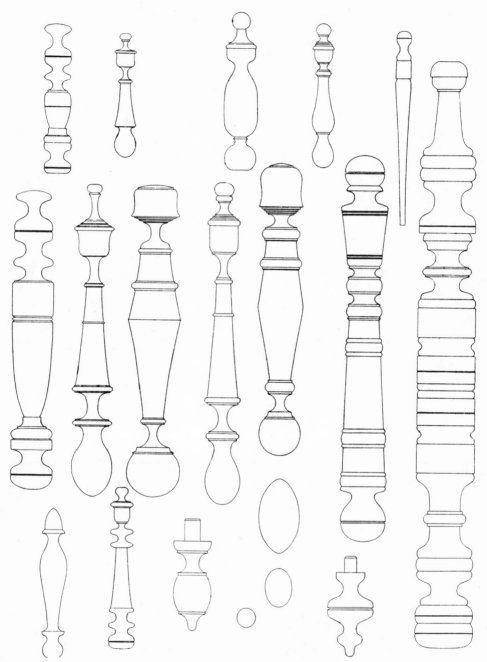

1054–1071. CUPBOARD AND CHEST AND TABLE DROPS. 17th CENTURY.

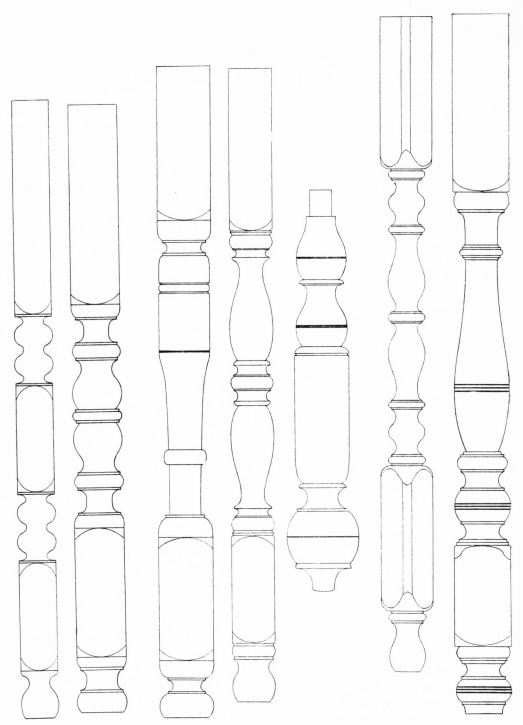

1072–1078. 17th Century Table and Couch Legs.

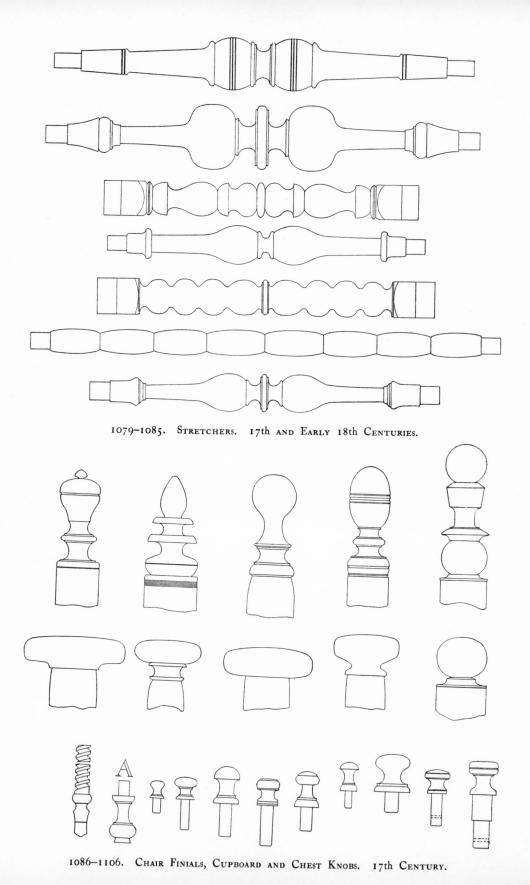

1079–1085. Stretchers. 17th and Early 18th Centuries.

1086–1106. Chair Finials, Cupboard and Chest Knobs. 17th Century.

1107–1111.   17th Century Table and Chair Legs.

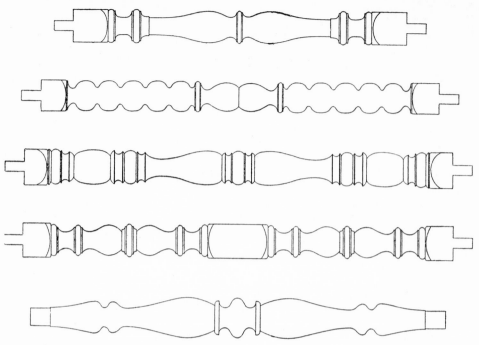

1112–1116. Table and Chair Stretchers. 17th and Early 18th Centuries.

1117–1119. 17th Century Court Cupboard Pillars.

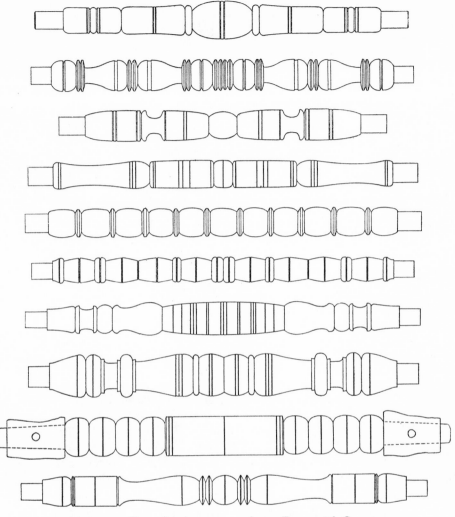

1120–1129. CHAIR STRETCHERS. 17th AND EARLY 18th CENTURIES.

Owner: Mr. Mark M. Henderson of Norwalk, Connecticut.

No. 1010. A looking-glass dating from about 1700. It is all original, but there was a decorative crest, which has been lost. We presume all the fine looking-glasses of the period to have had crests. Most of these, however, are now missing. The reason for this is that the crest was separately made and attached by dovetailed cleats on the back. It is not until we have the crest made as a unit with the glass that we begin to find such crests still attached quite generally. The glass in this frame is original. We do not know why this method of grinding ever went out. We understand there is some practical difficulty in grinding

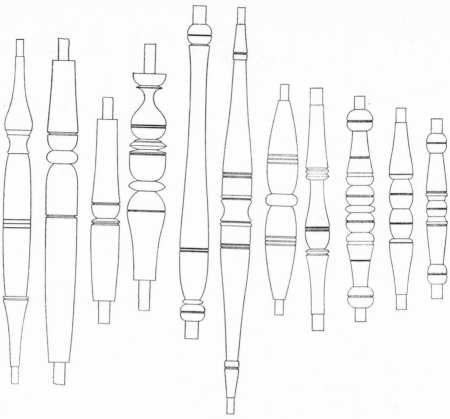

1130–1140.   Chair Spindles.   17th Century.

modern glasses in the same faces. The effort now is seemingly, by a sharp bevel, to emphasize the grinding. This is partly owing to the greater thickness of modern plate. In the old days, however, there was an effort made to hide the junction of the bevel with the main face of the glass.

It will be seen, as we proceed, that the earliest looking-glasses were nearly square. In this form the glass was less expensive. Later, for the same reason, we often have looking-glasses in two parts, with one glass under the other, a scheme devised for the same reason of economy.

We do not know how the ground bevel originated, nor why it was used. In this connection we should notice the shape of the earliest frames. They were very wide, like raised panels, and the molding retreats in a soft ovolo to the outside. This is directly opposite from the type of frame used about 1850.

Size: $27\frac{3}{4}$ by $31\frac{1}{4}$ inches outside. The glass is $18\frac{1}{4}$ by 22 inches. The wood is walnut veneer on pine, as usual.

1141–1149. Finials, Drops, and Stair Banisters. 17th Century.

No. 1011. This glass, also, evidently had a top which has been lost. The inlay here is very like that on No. 1009, only here it is visible. The inlay is in satin and tulip woods.

Size: The glass is 16 by 19¾ inches. The frame is 4 inches wide in addition. The width of this frame is important, as it indicates great age in this style of molding.

Owner: Mr. Francis Hill Bigelow.

No. 1012. This is the first instance of a looking-glass in which the cresting is an integral part of the frame. The decoration at the top, which shows indistinctly, is a very good inlaid design in tulip wood. The glass is not original. There were two glasses. The frame is walnut.

Date: 1710–1720.

Size: The width of the frame is here reduced from the other examples we have seen, indicating a later date and an increase in delicacy of treatment. It is 1¾ inches in width. The outside measurement of the frame is 18½ by 48½ inches. The adaptability of walnut for furniture making was recognized in the south of Europe at a period somewhat remote. All record of the matter is lost. In the early veneers it was sometimes too thick. It was laid on in cross sections, as in this frame, and the joints sometimes open. The modern method of the use of very thin veneer is designed partly for economy and partly from the supposition that the veneer will stand better. The tendency to curl is noticeable in most heavy veneers. The use of pine as a basis of veneers is proof positive that pine was commonly used, in English furniture at least, in this connection.

No. 1013. A walnut frame with convex molding. The style of the top is frequently seen in English looking-glasses. The pierced work sometimes outlines a design of heraldry. During the reign of William and Mary, when these glasses were made, the loyalty of the colonists was such that royal emblems might easily have been cut here. We remember such a loyal emblem in pine as the keystone of the finish of a window in a dwelling house in Portsmouth, New Hampshire, as late as 1760. But the builder was a Tory!

One should carefully distinguish between these fretted or pierced frames in walnut, of the period we are now treating, and the later scrolled and fretted frames of the Chippendale period, when the work was done on mahogany, and extended all about the looking-glass. In our period, the decoration is, for the most part, at the top. If this rule is transgressed, we find it at the top and bottom only, but never at the sides.

Size: Of glass, 11⅞ by 17⅛ inches.

Date: 1710–1730.

Owner: Mr. Francis Hill Bigelow.

1150–1153.   18th and 17th Century Chair Finials.

1154–1156.   17th Century Chair Finials.

1157–1163. HOUSEHOLD UTENSILS AND FROE. 18th CENTURY.

1164–1166. 17th CENTURY CHAIR FINIALS.

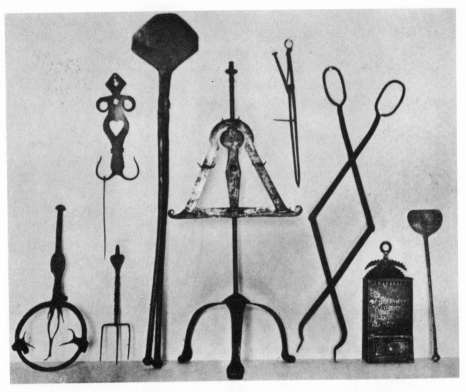

1167-1175.　Various Iron Utensils.　17th and 18th Centuries.

1176-1186.　Iron Utensils.　18th Century.

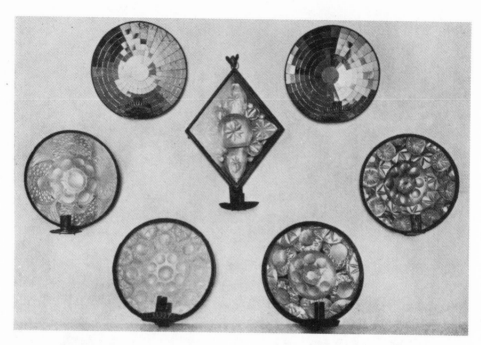

1187–1193. GLASS AND PEWTER SCONCE REFLECTORS. 18th CENTURY.

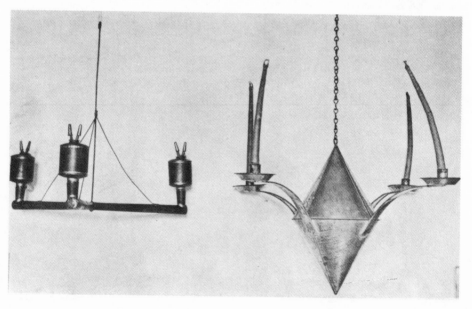

1194–1195. A LAMP AND A CANDLE CHANDELIER.

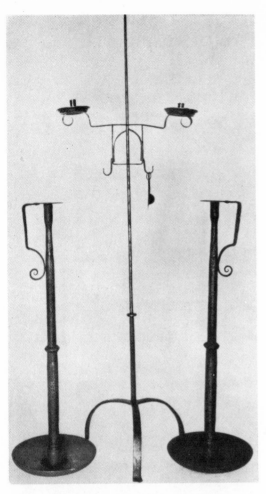

1196–1198. Floor Stand and Candle Sticks.

1199. Two Tier Chandelier.

1200–1205. Rush Lights and Lamps. 17th, 18th and 19th Centuries.

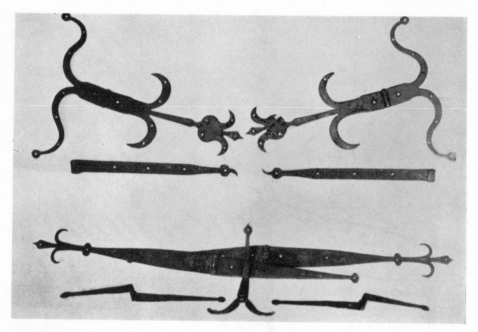

1206–1212. Tulip Blossom, Tulip Bud, Scrolled Chest and Buck Horn Hinges.

1213–1216. An Attic of 1752 with Various Furnishings.

No. 1014. A flat walnut frame. The glass is beautifully engraved, in the upper section, in a floral design, with birds and conventional scrolls. At this date the cutting of the upper glass in imitation of flowers and birds became popular. It would have seemed better to have left the glass free for the use originally intended in a looking-glass. We see, however, that the use of a looking-glass itself is in the direction of luxury, and invariably must accompany the development of taste and the ramifications of style.

A glass as large as this forms an important part of household decoration. The use of looking-glasses for this purpose from this point on is important. They not only served their original purpose, but added light and brilliance to the rooms in which they were placed.

Size: Of glass, $13\frac{7}{8}$ by $33\frac{7}{8}$ inches.

Date: About 1710.

Owner: Mr. Francis Hill Bigelow.

No. 1015. This frame is in a convex molding in burl walnut. One begins to see here the scrolled lines at the top, as we reach the Queen Anne period.

Size: $15\frac{3}{4}$ by $43\frac{1}{4}$ inches. The frame is $2\frac{1}{8}$ inches wide.

Date: About 1710.

Owner: Mr. Francis Hill Bigelow.

No. 1016. A walnut looking-glass in two parts. The bird cut in the upper glass is sometimes called a phoenix and sometimes a pheasant, but is not always recognizable by any of Audubon's illustrations. It is at least a bird, and a touch of mystery is rather an advantage. In this instance one sees clearly the method of the time, in lapping the upper glass over the lower. The object, of course, is to blend the two glasses as much as possible. It was at a later date that the division was frankly made by a section of the molding. In that case, the upper glass was often used to frame a design. Here the original idea still prevailed, of continuing the reflecting surfaces as a unit. The rabbet in the frame, into which the upper glass fitted, was made deeper; the rabbet in the lower section being more shallow, the glasses came together nicely. Old glasses, becoming a little shaky, are very likely to give trouble at this point, and permit the upper glass to slip down. Hence many were broken. The wood of this frame is somewhat bleached, showing how light walnut may gain a quite charming but very different color from that intended by the maker.

Size: The full hight is 37 inches.

Date: About 1710.

No. 1017. An interesting looking-glass, with painted section. The upper section is a panel of wood on which is represented a ship in full sail. The colors are now very quiet, but entirely distinct. All parts are original. We see here a tendency toward the abandonment of the use of the upper section as a looking-glass, giving it over to decoration entirely.

The use of wood as a ground for pictures is extremely early, some of the great paintings of the ages being done on wood. At first thought it seems not to be a suitable substance, yet the work done on it has often proved more permanent than that on canvas.

Date: About 1710.

Owner: Mr. Chauncey C. Nash.

No. 1019. A looking-glass which was, of course, designed to carry a sconce on the central projection at the bottom of the frame, which is very closely similar to the projections on the frame of No. 1008. The plain semi-circular top is unusual. Very narrow glasses of this character were often in pairs, and it is probable that this specimen once had a mate. One should compare the molded frame of this glass with a similar molding which runs around the backs of walnut chairs of the same period. The design was a favorite one of the cabinet makers of that day, who were also capable of getting into ruts, like those of the present time. " We refer," as the Rev. Dr. Hawes of Hartford used to say, " to those to whom we allude."

Size: $7\frac{1}{2}$ by $20\frac{1}{4}$ inches.

Date: 1700–1730.

Owner: Mr. Francis Hill Bigelow.

No. 1020. A looking-glass with a stained maple frame. Maple, as of less value than walnut, is more likely to indicate American origin when found in a looking glass. Nevertheless, we should be very careful of this conclusion. There is much maple in England and it was used more or less in furniture.

This glass, though rather simple, is of very pleasing design. The odd button ornament, or boss, and the somewhat wandering, uncertain lines of the scroll are interesting gropings after beauty.

Size: The narrow part of the frame is $1\frac{1}{8}$ inches, and is convex, as quite generally in this period. The glass is $11\frac{1}{4}$ by 17 inches.

Owner: Mr. Francis Hill Bigelow.

No. 1021. A warming-pan with an iron handle and a curved portion of the top to form a hook. These hooks were more often turned side-wise, and in the form of a shepherd's crook. The warming-pan with the iron handle is earlier than that with the wooden handle. One sees here the brass cover pierced in a decorative design.

No. 1022. A looking-glass with a handsomely scrolled crest. We like this type of scroll better than the usual pierced scrolls in the English looking-glass. Further, we are more inclined to believe in the American origin of looking-glasses with simple scrolls. The frame has the extraordinary width of $4\frac{1}{4}$ inches. The veneer is in apple wood, showing the end grain. In this case the glass is covered to avoid confusing reflections. Of course the glass is beveled.

It is the spirit of the true collector to value the glass as much as, or more than, the frame. He resists even the re-silvering of an old glass, yet many old glasses are re-silvered, but the result is not entirely satisfactory. It seems impossible to secure a perfect amalgam. Formerly, mercury was used in an alloy with tin. Pure silver is sometimes used. The direct rays of the sun would soon ruin the silvering on a glass. It is for this reason that old glasses passing through so many experiences are usually in so bad a condition. The suspicion arises that new plate is sometimes submitted to direct sunlight to secure the old effect. It is easy, however, by noticing the softness of the bevel on the old glasses, to distinguish them from the new.

Size: The glass is $15\frac{1}{2}$ by $18\frac{1}{4}$ inches.

Owner: Mr. Francis Hill Bigelow.

No. 1023. A looking-glass of Japanese design. The scroll is very tasteful. The glass is cut above in a foliage pattern.

Owner: Mr. L. G. Myers.

No. 1024. This so-called goose-yoke which is 9 inches long and has a large ring, is connected with the following tale, upon which the reader may pass his own judgment. It is said that a tame goose was yoked here with a wild goose which had been winged and caught for this purpose. The ring was then used to attach a cord, fastened to a stone thrown to the bottom of the goose pond, as a tether. The pair of geese could then sail about within a certain radius and served as a decoy for bringing down wild geese. The yoke is precisely like a reduced ox yoke. We have the single goose yoke, which is very commonly found. It is a triangular section.

Owner: Mr. Chetwood Smith.

Nos. 1025, 1026. These bedposts are believed to be of Spanish origin. We show them here because of the remarkable beauty of the turnings, which are found in almost identical form on some American chair finials. The wood of these posts is extremely gnarled, and difficult to work, so that below the frame it is left entirely rough, the thought being that as it was to be covered by a valance, it was not worth while to smooth. We show these turnings here as an interesting example of the universality of motives, at least in western Europe. These turnings may be suggested as indicating how, from the Spanish Netherlands, the turnings of the Brewster and Carver chairs may have come to America.

The large diameter of the turning is about 3 inches. The small diameter is about $1\frac{3}{8}$ inches, and the greatest length of a finial is about 10 inches.

No. 1027. A spinning jenny with the frame somewhat resembling that of a chair. This type is often found in Connecticut. There are, as one observes, two treadles which are intended to make the operation of the wheel simpler and steadier. Another feature of interest is that the spinning head, which hangs over the side of the frame, can be swung up out of the way by loosening the hand screw on the front of the frame; also, whenever it is set for spinning, it can be given just the proper tension by the set of the screw.

No. 1028. A wrought maple leaf latch. This remarkable and handsome example, no fellow of which we have so far seen, was probably intended for use on a cupboard door, as it is molded on the edge, apparently to match the mold on such a door. It is supposed to have caught by a snap, and to have been reversed from the usual latch position on this account. Size: $5\frac{1}{2}$ by 9 inches.

TURNINGS

CAREFULLY outlined drawings which were done on a full size scale, and reduced, are here exhibited. They will give an accurate idea of most of the forms in which the furniture of our period was turned. All but one of these drawings were done from the furniture. That one was done from a photograph on which we had the dimensions.

Nos. 1029–1033. The posts on court cupboards. No. 1029 is the upper post in the Parmenter cupboard.

Size: $20\frac{1}{8}$ by 4 inches, the latter dimension being the square of the top. The large part of the turning is only $\frac{1}{16}$ inch short of this dimension; the smallest is $1\frac{5}{8}$ inches.

Nos. 1030 and 1032 are the humbler turnings of pine court cupboards. No. 1031 is the reversible turning of the Prince-Howes cupboard. The turnings on the other cupboards of this style all vary somewhat from this one, but they are all about the same size. The size of this turning is $17\frac{3}{4}$ by $4\frac{7}{16}$ inches. The smallest diameter is $1\frac{3}{8}$ inches.

No. 1033 is the post of the Connecticut sunflower and tulip cupboard. These posts are practically the same on all the cupboards, with one exception. In fact, their similarity is so great that they are more like modern products in the sense of being almost interchangeable.

Nos. 1034–1037 are the heavy legs of the earliest tables. No. 1034 is the bulbous leg of the great Andover square table.

Size: $31\frac{3}{4}$ by $4\frac{1}{8}$ inches. The smallest diameter is $1\frac{3}{8}$ inches. The square of the leg is only $2\frac{3}{4}$ inches. At the top one sees the extension, which is a tenon entering into the mortise in the table top, which is, however, left unpinned so as to permit of lifting off the top.

Nos. 1036–1037 are respectively the legs of the Sudbury and the Salisbury communion tables. Each has a diameter of $3\frac{1}{2}$ inches.

Nos. 1038–1042 are table legs which come more in the range of common experience. No. 1038 is the leg of a trestle-board gate-table.

Size: 26 by $2\frac{5}{8}$ inches.

The other turnings on this plate are all gate-leg table legs.

Nos. 1043–1048 are legs of various pieces. No. 1043 is the oak post of a chest-on-frame. No. 1044 is the oak leg of an early tavern table. No. 1045 is from a gate-leg table. No. 1046 is the post of an American turned settee. No. 1047 is the raked oak leg of a tavern table, and No. 1048 is the raked oak leg of a stool table.

Nos. 1049–1053 are the legs of the William and Mary and Queen Anne period, of the highboy and lowboy type, except that No. 1053 is the leg of a stool having a cross stretcher.

Nos. 1054–1071 are cupboard and chest half spindle turnings, drops, and bosses.

Nos. 1072–1078 are table, desk, or couch legs. No. 1076 is a very fine representation of the best type of the Pennsylvania turning, showing the ball of the foot larger than the rest of the turning, and the so-called blunt arrow with which the leg terminates at the floor. The chaise longue from which it is taken is in the author's collection. Heavy turnings like these are called fat. The ball of the foot is $3\frac{5}{16}$ inches in diameter.

Nos. 1079–1085 are the stretchers of chairs, the first two being especially heavy and fine, and such as are found on the best types of the Pennsylvania chairs, or on the ram's horn arm New England type. The No. 1080 is $3\frac{5}{16}$ inches, whereas the smallest diameter comes down to $\frac{7}{8}$ of largest diameter of the turning on No. 1079 is $2\frac{11}{16}$ inches, and that on an inch on this latter piece.

Nos. 1086–1106 represent, on the upper row, the finials of seventeenth century chairs, though No. 1086 was probably not found until the very end of the century, and is a distinct decline from the others. No. 1087 is one of the best Pilgrim turnings, and No. 1090 is the oddest turning. Nos. 1091 to 1095 represent the mushrooms on the front posts of chairs, except the last which is the conventional ball on most Pilgrim chairs before the mushroom period.

Nos. 1096 to 1106 show the knobs on drawers and doors of the period, though the first is a flat-headed screw for a candle stand, and the next is the foot of a desk box, and the last is a knob running through a cupboard door, and having an inside button attached.

Nos. 1107–1111. Chair legs, No. 1108 being the oak leg of the X stretcher Jersey chair table. Its large diameter is $2\frac{3}{8}$ inches. No. 1109 is the leg of the Robinson wainscot chair.

Nos. 1112–1116 are table stretchers, except the last, which is a chair-rung of a New England type.

Nos. 1117–1119. The first is the walnut post of a court cupboard from Durham, Connecticut. Most likely it should be reversed. It is not so fine a type as most others on court cupboards. No. 1118 is a court cupboard table leg, $3\frac{1}{2}$ inches in diameter. No. 1119 is the bulbous turning of the Virginia court cupboard. Just above and just below the great bulb there is a dowel. This central section of the turning is 6 inches in diameter, and 8 inches long.

Nos. 1120–1129 are Brewster, Carver, and mushroom chair rails. These are among the most interesting of all.

Nos. 1130–1140 are the spindles of beds and chairs; mostly, of course, of chairs. The five short turnings at the right are all back spindles of Carver chairs.

Nos. 1141–1149 are miscellaneous turnings, the second line of four above one another being the drops or finials of seventeenth century stairs, and the next two in line being seventeenth century banisters. Nos. 1148 and 1149 are finials on the cross stretchers of lowboys.

Nos. 1150–1153. Photographs of finials, the first two being of chairs of the date of 1700 or thereabouts, and the last two being from a Brewster and a Carver. The diameters of the last two are a little more than $2\frac{1}{2}$ inches. Before the shrinkage they were probably $2\frac{5}{8}$ inches.

Nos. 1154–1156. These are turnings on Carver chairs, except the last, which is from a Pilgrim slat back. Sizes, in their larger diameters, are $2\frac{1}{2}$ inches.

Nos. 1157–1163. These illustrate household utensils. The shovel is wrought from one piece and has a curled-over handle. It rests on a great mortar which is all a man can lift. The little handled tool in front of it is called a froe. It was used to split clapboards. A stick of oak about 16 inches in diameter and 4 feet long, and of very straight grain, was stood on end and marked at the center. The froe was then set with its point at the center and was struck with a maul or an ax successively as the froe was moved about the circle, as we would cut minute pieces of pie — war-wedges, so to speak. This accounts for the thinning of the clapboard from the butt: The clapboards were then roughly shaved to remove any prominent ridges of the grain. Some dwellings still remain with these clapboards in place, where protected by a lean-to roof on the back.

Nos. 1164–1166. Chair finials of the Carver and Brewster type. Shown here in half-size.

WROUGHT IRON IN AMERICA

WITHIN a recent period much interest has been aroused in this subject. The author has sought far and wide for all good specimens of wrought iron. He has not confined himself to the earliest types. We have hinges which probably date from 1640, and possibly a few latches from the same period. The best period of wrought iron was not, strangely enough, the seventeenth century, nor even the early eighteenth century, although we have many remarkable pieces included within those dates. Some of these pieces are also, owing to their rarity or quaintness, very much to be desired. If, however, we consider the subject fully from the standpoint of style and design, we should say that from the time of the Revolution to the end of the eighteenth century was the best period. After 1800 there was a rapid decline, except in Pennsylvania. There the traditions of the blacksmiths continued. We find, astonishing to relate, that good Betty lamps, which are classed in Pennsylvania under the large term fat lamps, in the same category with standing fat lamps, were made up to and beyond the middle of the nineteenth century!

In our treatment of this subject, we make no apologies for having scattered through the work, in the nature of small cuts at the bottoms of pages, a good many specimens of iron, which could not otherwise be included. We have sought to make the showing of lamps in iron and in tin as full as our resources permitted. We have excluded all except one or two fortuitous pieces of pewter, not that the subject lacks interest, but because of our limitations and the fact that other publications discuss that branch of household decoration.

We exclude from our lists the cast latches which came in about 1835. They are neither good in themselves nor in sufficient variety to attract attention. We exclude also, almost entirely, brass latches and other fixtures, because that is a large department of its own, and merits separate treatment. Indeed, brass has been thought of sufficient importance to feature largely and continuously in the work of the best English makers.

The fine and characteristic American wrought latches and hinges, however, went out completely from use and from the attention of American architects and decorators. In this department we have sought to give a very much fuller setting forth of those subjects than has hitherto been attempted.

Nos. 1167–1175. A series of articles belonging to Mrs. J. Insley Blair. The heart motive skewer holder, from which one skewer hangs, is the best we have seen. It is dated 1729. These skewer holders are now much sought for. The highest piece on the plate is an odd shaped waffle iron, and dates 1748. The three-pronged fork is inlaid with brass initials " J. D.", and with a star.

The large central piece, a spit on a rod, has a foreign aspect but it is supposedly American. The next two pieces are pipe tongs. The pipe box of tin carries a legend " Peter Thatcher, Yarmouth, Aug. the 28, 1813." It is the only pipe box we know with a legend, or constructed of tin.

Nos. 1176–1186. Utensils in the collection of Mr. Francis Mireau. On the left is a crude early thermometer. The spiraled trivet is interesting. The horn shaped affair was to hook to the belt and insert the whetting iron, which lies below. The grapples are said to have been used in fishing the old oaken bucket out of the well when it cast loose from its moorings. There is a shaving mug of tin, a couple of odd shaped choppers and a Colonial rat trap!

Nos. 1187–1193. A remarkable series of sconces in glass and decorative stamped pewter forms, owned by Mrs. J. Insley Blair. The diamond shaped sconce is exceedingly rare, if not unique. All the others are much sought for and at the present time the pewter discs, which are covered with glass to prevent them from tarnishing, are almost as much cherished by owners as the style of the two at the top which are made in glass.

Nos. 1194 and 1195. Two chandeliers belonging to Mrs. J. Insley Blair. That on the left is for lard oil and is three-branched. That on the right, for candles, is most quaint in shape, the central portion or hub being formed of two cones, the bases of which are attached to one another.

Nos. 1196–1198. This pair of candle sticks is said to have been found in the ruins of a church in Manheim, Pennsylvania. They are unlike almost anything else that we find in America, but we judge them to be a true Pennsylvania product.

The tall candle stand is a good piece of a type fairly well established.

No. 1199. A double chandelier owned by Mrs. J. Insley Blair. This quaint piece, painted yellow, is said to have been taken from a church in Hebron, Connecticut. The church was built in 1762. The crenelated crown-like circles of different sizes, are very tastefully done, together with the scalloped shaped canopy. Tin chandeliers are now highly regarded. Not many of them remain, especially in as good a form as this example.

Nos. 1200–1205. A series of lighting fixtures owned by Mr. Anthony T. Kelley of Springfield. It is a mooted question whether the rush light

1217–1223. Sconces and Lamps. 18th Century.

1224–1233. Lamps and Candle Sticks. 17th and 18th Centuries.

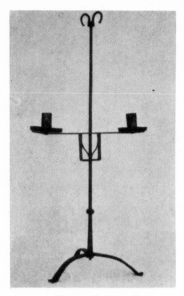

1234. TABLE CANDLE STAND.   1235. TABLE CANDLE STAND.

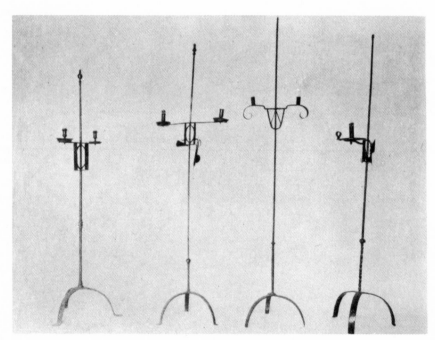

1236–1239. FOUR FLOOR STANDS WITH DOUBLE BRACKETS. 18th CENTURY.

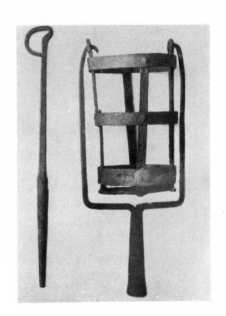

1240–1241.   Beacon Holders and Toddy Iron.

1242.   Clock Work Jack.

1243.   A Post Lantern.

1244–1245. MOLDED BRASS BOX LOCK, STRIKER RESTORED. 1730–60.

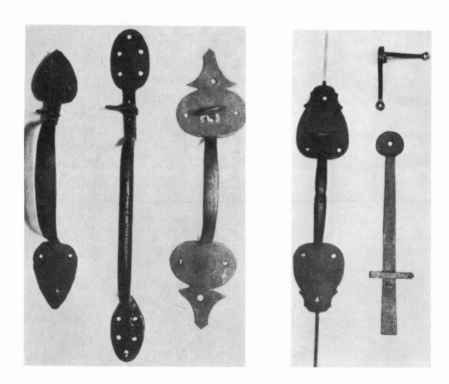

1246–1250. FOUR LATCHES AND DOUBLE BRACED STRIKER.

holders were made in America. The two examples here are the first in the row, and the next to the last. It will be seen that the first has an iron tripod base, and the next to the last has a decorated wooden base.

In each case the arm which opens the nippers is a weight to hold them together with sufficient pressure so that the rush light shall not fall, but can easily be raised as it burns. We see no reason why these rush light holders should not have been made in America. The rushes were common and the use of the holders abroad was common. Of course, there was a greater abundance here, at least after the very first years, of tallow for candles, and of oils. We hardly believe the frugal Pennsylvania and Yankee settlers would have failed to provide their own holders, had they wanted them. It is possible that they were very little used in America. We are bound to say, however, that so far as we are able to trace any of these holders at all, they are traced to Europe. The other oil or fat burning lights in this row are sufficiently self-explanatory.

Nos. 1206–1212. These hinges, designed with a good deal of taste, are from Pennsylvania, except the single buck horn which was found in Massachusetts.

The tulip blossom hinge is the best example that has come to our attention, although we have recently seen a sketch of another almost as good. In this hinge we have the fully developed blossom, which the reader is asked to compare with the subsequent examples of the bud, and with the examples of the bud, the half opened blossom and the fully opened blossom used in various latches. We have not found a fully developed latch with a blossom as good as this and of large size. We think it quite probable, however, that such a latch existed. The long chest hinges in a fine fleur-de-lis pattern are also from Pennsylvania. There is an oddity about these hinges which may deceive the collector. Their edges were shaped by filing, and we can personally vouch for the fact that some hinges known to have been in place for at least one hundred years show the bright marks of the file on the edges, whereas the main surface has an oxidized appearance. It is known that filed surfaces retain their brightness longer than hammered surfaces. There is a great variety of designs in Pennsylvania chest hinges. Some of them which we shall show, are very attractive. There is scarcely any end, however, to the ramifications of design in this department of hardware. This fact is the more curious, since in the seventeenth century the chest hinges were quite simple, generally merely staples, otherwise called loops.

Nos. 1213–1216. The attic of the Webb-Welles house, Wethersfield, Connecticut, now open to the public. It was photographed as the author found it, except, perhaps, for the addition of a chair or two. Curious lanterns are hung about, together with herbs. There is a gallery, a small portion of which shows, which is reached by an open stair. People there could witness dancing on the main floor of the attic. The house dates from 1752.

Nos. 1217–1223. A series of lighting fixtures belonging to Mrs. J. Insley Blair. Above are plain sconces, which nevertheless are very rare, with their three candle sockets each. The sconce below, with a reflector, is somewhat of a puzzle, as it would seem that a reflector was needed directly above each candle. The other reflecting sconces are better known, being more or less typical, but are now highly regarded. The next to the last in line is roughly shaped in tin to represent a sunburst. The middle piece, with a long post, has a handle showing a series of candle sockets around it, and is most rare and attractive. It will be noted that we do not attempt to date these pieces very precisely. Doubtless some come down from the seventeenth century. Most of them are of the eighteenth century and a few, no doubt, date from the earlier part of the 19th c.

Nos. 1224–1233. The first piece is an extremely rare standard for Betty lamps, arranged with a crossbar and screw. It is important. The lamp to the right on the bottom is a cast Betty lamp, corresponding to the wrought sort next it to the right. At the top in the center is a light trammel with a most quaint device attached.

The standard to the right of it is of turned wood, another example of which we show. It has upon it, however, an earthenware open Betty lamp, which is extraordinarily rare.

The combined rush and candle holder at the right is of great interest.

No. 1234. A candle stand of iron on tripod feet, with a handle at the top roughly scrolled like a buck horn. The crossbar is adjustable. This is one of the rarest pieces we have ever seen, and it has great interest because it is a table type, the same general pattern as the tall iron floor stand.

The hight is 22 inches, and the outside measurement of the bar and attached saucers is $10\frac{3}{8}$ inches. The feet are scrolled in simple pattern.

It was found in Guilford, Connecticut.

Owner: Mrs. J. Insley Blair.

No. 1235. An adjustable table stand for two candles. The material of the post is iron, very nicely wrought, but terminated with a turned brass ring, the base of which is milled. The turned base of the whole affair is weighted and the reflectors as well as the candle bar are adjustable. An extinguisher is caught in a little socket provided for it. This was found in Boston.

Owner: Mr. John H. Halford.

Nos. 1236–1239. Four floor stands for candles, three of which have the conventional adjustable crossbar for two candles, while the last, on the right, has an adjustable bracket for one candle.   The third stand in line terminates with an iron finial hammered from the bow of the post, and the fillet lower on the post is also hammered.   In the case of the other examples the attached portions at the finial and on the stand are of brass.

No. 1240.   A torch-holder which was found on the North Shore, but of whose origin, of course, we are ignorant.   It swings on hinged sockets and is scrolled with English designs, but we believe it to have been long in America.

No. 1241.   Two articles, the left-hand one being a toddy iron.   One should distinguish between such toddy irons and the goffering irons which were toddy irons only by accommodation.

The other article illustrated under this number is a torch holder which was attached to a pole, and which swivels.   We name this article, like the preceding, a torch holder, but undoubtedly pitch pine was placed in the iron basket.   The name may be as good as any.

No. 1242.   An iron and brass clockwork jack, to which a pulley is attached to turn the spit rod which rests upon the andirons, to roast the meat.   We had always supposed these pieces to be American.   We have found two of iron and a third one in which the mandrel was of wood, all on the North Shore.   We have lately seen one of the same pattern that has come from England.   These pieces have at the top a kind of balance wheel, which was spun by hand when it was desired to start the jack.   The weight was so accurately balanced that it was intended to run slowly.   A worm gear is attached to the hand wheel.

These articles are among the most interesting and curious that remain to us from the older day, so that a fireplace fitted with them is of the greatest interest.   At the Essex Institute, Salem, a fireplace is so equipped.

We have also seen one at the Hancock House, Lexington, and at the Wayside Inn, South Sudbury, and the author has one.   There are probably others.

The mechanism is earlier than the clockwork jack invented by Simon Willard.   It is said that Queen Victoria's meat was cooked in Windsor Castle on a jack similar to this, which has been in use there from time immemorial.

No. 1243.   A lantern to be set upon a post.   It is of very good early design and terminates with a finial of turned wood.

Nos. 1244–1245.   A brass box lock which, owing to its material, is somewhat of an intruder in this work.   The author found the original in Portsmouth, New Hampshire.   Afterwards he found a similar one among the unlisted treasures of the Metropolitan Museum.   The striker and the key are new.   The molding of the lock is the unusual and meritorious feature.   Such locks were in use from about 1725 through the century.

Nos. 1246–1248. Wrought iron latches, the central one of which is 16 inches long and only 1¾ inches in width. It is on this account that it has five perforations for nailing. Undoubtedly it was set on a very narrow stile, and it was difficult to attach such a latch on a narrow plate so that it would be secure. The left-hand latch is of a somewhat crude heart shape, and that on the right is a ball and blunt spear design.

Nos. 1249–1250. An unusual latch, the spear of the top of which is broken, but faintly outlined. It was 19¾ inches long and 3¼ inches wide. The matter of most interest in relation to it is the catch, which may be seen to be braced by a scroll turning in two ways. We have seen several of these. It shows feeling for design and yet, perhaps, not a very early date.

Nos. 1251–1256. A series of latches of somewhat unusual interest. The first we may call a ball and diamond. The second is a scroll design apparently unnamed. The third and largest is one of half a dozen we have seen. It is 14½ inches long. The fifth in line is a tulip partly opened, and more opened at the top than at the bottom. The last is a tulip bud.

Nos. 1257–1268. A series of latch bars. The one at the bottom is no less than 25 inches long. The second in line is finished at the top in a spiraled cone. Its total length is 15 inches. With one exception, this is the most remarkable which we have seen. It was found in Pennsylvania, as was also the fourth from the right. This seems to have been the suggestion of the Pennsylvania locks with a hollowed ball. The third from the left must have had its lifting disc run through a slot in the door. The fifth in line is the latest form of latch that can be considered passable. It has the plate to attach it to the door. All early forms are nailed simply. This piece has a little lifting ball riveted to the latch bar, which is also another late type. The long latch at the top came from a church door and passed through a slot in the wood, which accounts for its opposite form. It has a fine spiral. It is 23 inches long at the hinged portion.

The origin is Connecticut.

Nos. 1269–1272. The left-hand latch is of a crude, simple pattern. The next is a curious, rather than an elegant design. The third is very like No. 1249, except that it is made without the spear terminals. The last is a somewhat crude ball and spear.

Nos. 1273–1275. The first latch is the heart pattern, and the second is of a less perfectly shaped heart. The last latch is the triangular pattern. There is shown at the top the ordinary simplest form of the catch or striker, which is always of a square taper section, driven into the jamb. Below are shown the faces or sides of the thumb pieces.

No. 1276. A latch belonging to Mr. L. P. Goulding, another of

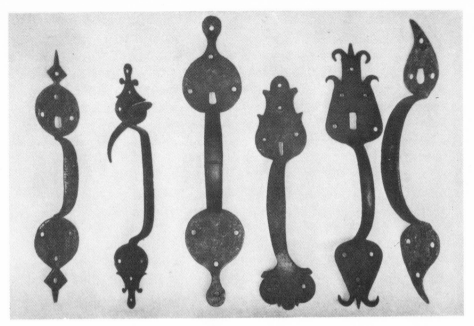

1251–1256. Six Interesting Latches. 18th Century.

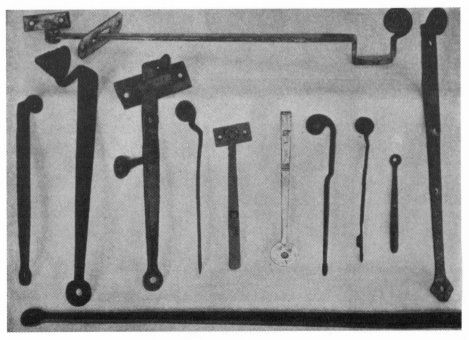

1257–1268. Twelve Styles of Latch Bars.

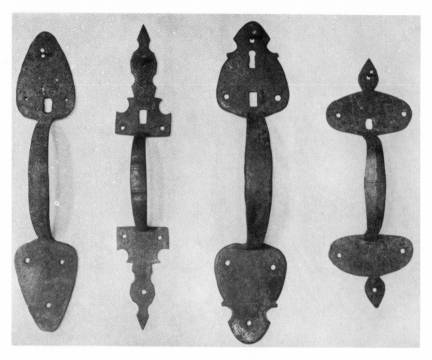

1269–1272. FOUR LATCHES. 18th CENTURY.

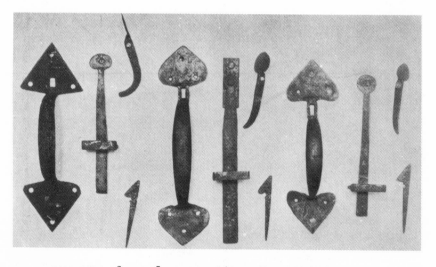

1273–1275. SIMPLE LATCHES. 18th AND EARLY 19th CENTURIES.

1276–1278. Latches and a Betty Lamp.

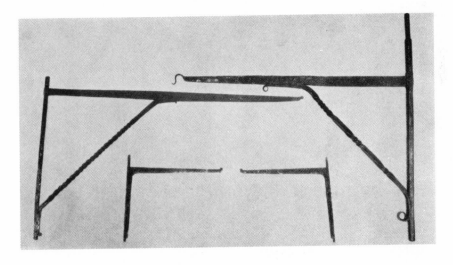

1279–1280. Cranes of Various Styles.

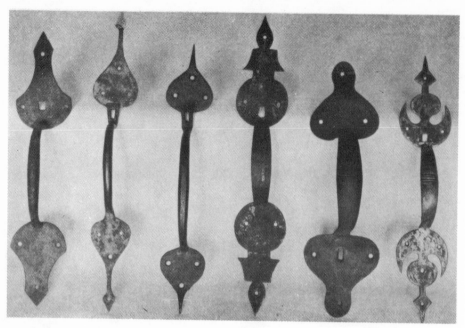

1281–1286. Six Scrolled Latches. 18th Century.

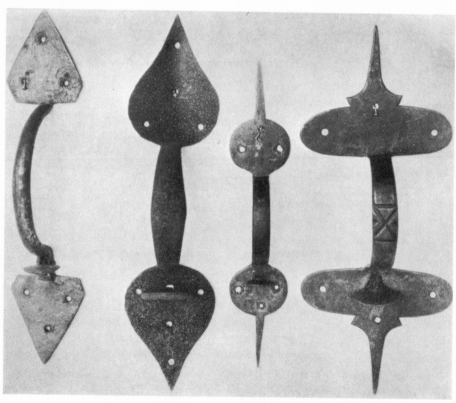

1287–1290. Four Scrolled Latches. 18th Century.

which is owned by the writer. It is a very good pattern called the ball and spear.

Nos. 1277–1278. An elaborate and important latch belonging to Mr. H. W. Erving. It is not always possible, nor perhaps necessary, that we should name these shapes, but we delight to try. In this case, however, we admit ourselves at a loss. At the right is a Betty lamp.

Nos. 1279–1280. A series of cranes. The small ones show a pair to be used one on either side of the same fireplace, and therefore is permissibly small. The large crane with an ornamental end and a spiraled brace originated in Pennsylvania. The other spiral crane is a New England piece. We would hazard the judgment that the frequent use of large trammels in Pennsylvania indicates their use on a lug pole rather than a crane.

The varieties of cranes are numerous. Their use is later than that of the lug pole, which was fixed in the fireplace at a point far above the lintel. It was not possible to swing out a kettle. The removal of a kettle was therefore a very awkward matter, and somewhat dangerous, the heat of the fire being intense unless one waited for it to die down, as was not desirable in the winter. The hanging of the crane symbolizes the setting. up of a household, and the gallantry of the young husband, to enable his wife to swing out the pot where she could manipulate it without scorching her face.

Nos. 1281–1286. A series of six latches, some of which are quite important. The second is a very delicate heart pattern, with an attenuated spear point. The third is the pointed heart pattern. The fourth, we suppose, might be named from some flower, but we leave that matter to the botanists.

The size is 16½ by 2⅞ inches. It was bought in New York.

The last in line is a handsome pattern of extreme rarity.

Nos. 1287–1290. The left-hand example is merely a triangular plate with the corners cut off. The next is a crude heart pattern, and the third is a small ball and spear design. The last in line is one of the best we know for design, being of a flattened ball shape with the spear. One notices the ornamental cutting on the handle. In this connection, one should observe the handle decorations, because the style depends a good deal upon their character.

No. 1291. This might perhaps be called a thistle pattern. It is the most elaborate design we know. While only 14 inches in length, it succeeds in concentrating a good deal of decoration in a small space.

No. 1292 is a very large and simple latch, probably intended for a public door.

No. 1293 is said to be from a church door in Connecticut. It is 23 inches in length and while not elaborate, is a very dignified piece.

No. 1294 is the largest latch we have seen in an ornamental pattern. It is 26 inches in length and might perhaps be called a swordfish design. The spike at the top is hammered to a tapering cone. No doubt this also is a church door latch.

While foreign latches and hinges are, to a very great degree, more elaborate than our own, they would seem very inappropriate on American doors. Where they have been brought over and affixed to our doors they are much out of place. The charm of hardware is in its agreement with the simple architectural lines of the eighteenth century. Foreign hardware is spoiled by attachment to American doors, and the doors themselves are spoiled.

The thumb pieces of latches are sometimes held from dropping out of the throat or mortise through which they pass by splitting the section on the inside of the door, and swinging it out on a curve, making a kind of cusp. The other method is to attach it by an iron pin or dowel, passing through the throat and the thumb piece. We are inclined to believe the split thumb piece to be the older form. The thumb pieces are sometimes more or less elaborate, but in every case they should curl at the end and, in the best instances, a secondary short spiral terminates them. The small straight inside termination, such as we see on doors after 1800, gives no purchase by which to open the door, and we are often at a loss to know how they could have been used.

Nos. 1295–1299. The two examples on the left are Pennsylvania wrought combined locks and latches, the first with a rolled scroll and the second with a hollowed thumb piece. These latches spring. The third example is that of a native chest lock as found in Pennsylvania. It was attached on the interior. Some say these locks are foreign. Others maintain that they were made in Pennsylvania. They are very much like the intricately elaborate etched locks of Spain, except that they are simpler.

No. 1300 is one of two known. It is curious rather than elegant. The origin is Connecticut.

No. 1301 is another example of the ball and spear, with a looped latch bar.

Nos. 1302–1309. A series of eight latches, two of which are closely like others shown, whereas the fourth in line is a good type of the simple large heart latch. It has good design on the handle. The third from the right has the points turned over to be struck into the door when the latch is attached, and thus to form a secondary and additional means of rigidity. The second from the right is the simplest and commonest form of the latch as used at the last of the eighteenth and well into the nineteenth century, in which the plate is a simple disc or thumb-shaped piece. Many of these are still in place on houses of the period. Quite generally the thumb-piece is held in place by a pin. The last latch on the right is interesting because the handle is beveled, showing three faces.

Nos. 1310–1313. The left-hand latch shown here is possibly a reminiscence of a tulip bud, but we should rather call it a roll-pointed triangle. The example at the right has the fleur-de-lis above a ball at the top, and at the bottom an outline and an incised heart, of which we have noted no other examples. It was purchased in New York.

Its length is 17½ inches.

We elaborate later the use of the heart motive in hardware in matched sets for doors.

Nos. 1314–1318. Five latches, the first being a broad heart, the next a pointed heart, the third a rough triangle, the fourth a rather carefully outlined heart, and the last being the rare tulip pattern. We have the beginning of the opening of the bud below and a somewhat later stage above. This should be compared with No. 1255 and also with No. 1256 and other tulip bud patterns.

No. 1319 is a large and elaborate latch owned by Dr. Irving P. Lyon of Buffalo, New York. We may call it a swordfish design. The length of the entire handle plate is 24½ inches; of the handle proper, 8⅝ inches; of the latch bar, 17 inches. The measurement around the curves of the handle is 8⅝ inches, and the length of the spike is 5½ inches. The origin of the latch is not certain, but it is known to be American, and it probably came from Connecticut.

The special and perhaps unique design of the latch bar is very handsome. The catch also is braced by two scrolls, practically at right angles. It is all in all, perhaps, the most important example that has come to our attention.

Nos. 1322–1323. A large latch found in western Massachusetts, in which the ball element is repeated and the plate is terminated in a pointed triangular section. The scrolls cut to parallel the balls are a highly decorative feature. The thumb piece is of good design. The bar is flattened and scrolled at its inside termination beyond the ball. The guard, the bar, and the handle have the repeated molding to unite them in motive.

The size is 23 by 4¼ inches.

No. 1324 is the long section of a Pennsylvania chest lock, a kind of cock's comb.

Owner: Mrs. Edgar Munson of Williamsport, Pennsylvania, who has this hinge on an original Pennsylvania chest.

Nos. 1325–1326. A skewer holder with the original skewers. No doubt the skewer, being a small article, was quite likely to be mislaid. In well-regulated households, therefore, a skewer holder was hooked on the beam.

Nos. 1327–1328.   A small trammel with Betty lamp base attached. This is a quaint and unusual piece owned by Mr. H. W. Erving.

Nos. 1329–1331.   The pair of andirons on the left is an unusual American form.   The rings are more common in English examples.   On the right there are two single irons showing types of andirons, one with a bend over cone, the other with a scroll and disc.   The piece in the foreground was an ash bar to place before a small chimney fireplace.   There are four spirals at the corners to prevent its falling over, as it is flat and set on edge.   The pieces with rings are two forms of griddles, both swiveled.   At the right of them is a small charcoal stove.

Nos. 1332–1339.   It is a great pleasure to find and to show so many different types of trammels.   Until recently these interesting articles have been very much neglected.   That which is dated 1697 is the oldest dated piece of iron we have seen of this kind, and also the quaintest and the largest.   We therefore regard it more highly than any other.   It could not have been used except on a lug pole about nine feet above the floor, in order to hang the great kettle on the hook at the base and have it come above a backlog.   The etchings or scrolls have been filled with chalk in order to permit their outlines being discerned.

Next on the right is a chain trammel, the hight of which was changed by the use of the small hook at the top.   All the links of this chain are twisted and the large hook at the bottom is elaborately etched on its outside.

The long trammel to the right of this has the heart motive and is quite ornate and attractive.   It is all original except the wooden handle at the top, which had been lost or burned.   It of course was used to change the hight of the trammel.

On the extreme left of the page is a very unusually shaped trammel with wrought scroll.   The very short trammel has a heart shaped dated and initialed scroll quite like that found on a Betty lamp to be shown later.   The other trammels with holes and hooks are the more ordinary sort, but all those shown here have some especial merit.

Trammels give much character to a fireplace, especially those in the serrated form.   Of course, they are adapted only to the larger fireplaces. They connect us with the earliest period of fire making known to our branch of the race.   The trammel of 1697, when extended to its full length, was about 80 inches long.   Some of the chain trammels are almost as long.   A great fireplace with its series of chains and trammels was most impressive.   Trammels are very common still in Pennsylvania, but in New England they are rare, especially in their finer forms.   The writer

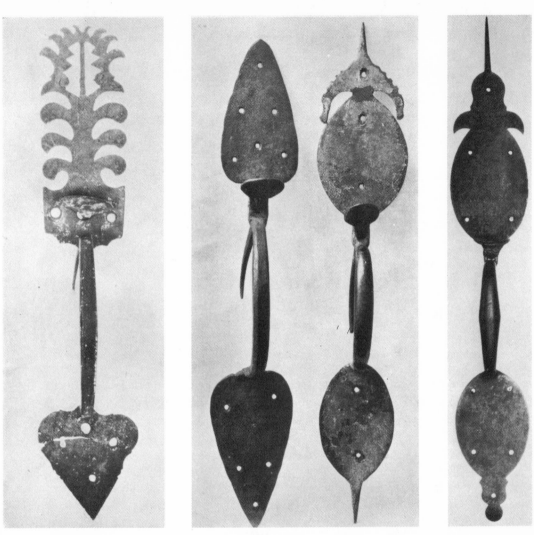

1291–1294. Flower Blossom Latch and Three Church Door Latches. 18th Century.

1295–1299. Five Pennsylvania Locks. 18th Century.

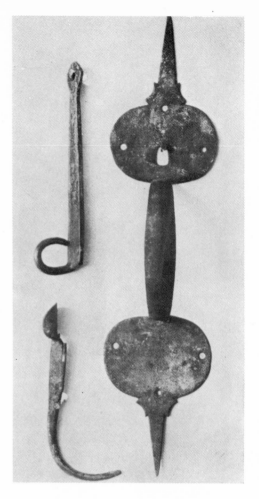

1300. Quaint Church Latch.

1301. Ball and Spear Latch.

1302–1309. 18th and Early 19th Century Wrought Latches.

1310–1313. Rolled Triangle, Heart and Fleur De Lis Latches. 18th Century.

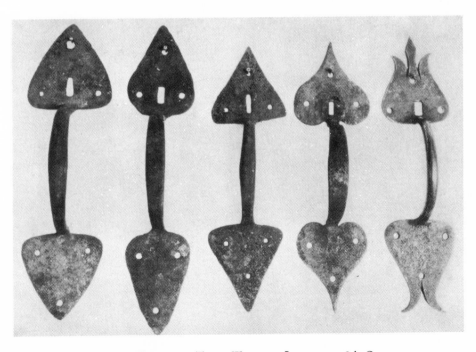

1314–1318. Heart and Tulip Wrought Latches. 18th Century.

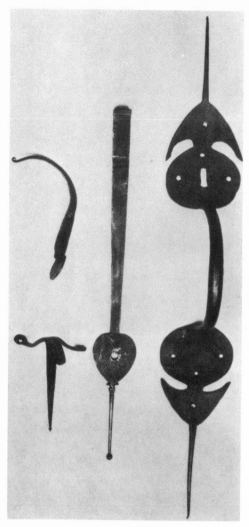

1319–21. SWORDFISH LATCH.

1322–23. DECORATIVE LATCH.

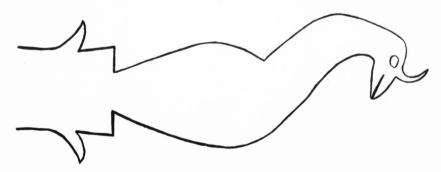

1324. BIRD HEAD HINGE, PENNSYLVANIA CHEST. 18th CENTURY.

has searched far and wide to obtain the fullest possible showing compatible with our space.

No. 1340. A trencher of curly maple, 13 by 14 inches. The shrinkage is shown by the difference in diameter. It proves that these pieces were turned while they were green. Such a trencher, together with great burl bowls and smaller trenchers, one at each plate on a trestle-board, is an assemblage of articles that transports us at once into the Middle Ages, and affords a fine rich old flavor to human life.

No. 1341. A reflector composed of small decorated pewter discs set behind a sealed glass to prevent tarnish.

No. 1342. A Betty or fat lamp on a four-legged stand. All parts of this piece are beautifully wrought and the Betty lamp itself is most carefully done. The lamp is adjustable. The hook of the shaft at the top was, of course, for a handle. The hight is just under two feet. The saucer base is $7\frac{1}{4}$ inches in diameter. The feet are welded into a unit and a hand bolt attaches them to the stand and the stand to the saucer. A table lamp of rare merit.

Nos. 1343–1347. On the left, a simple pair of pipe tongs, $25\frac{1}{2}$ inches long and coming to a very delicate point. The fork and spoon are highly attenuated and are in the hight of the modern fashion! The spoon is ornamented with a delicate fillet and a hook. The ladle is all wrought, and has two pouring nozzles. The piece on the right is a flatiron holder. The two pieces at the right are owned by Mr. L. P. Goulding.

No. 1348 is a heart shaped skewer holder of very interesting design, it being stamped with entwined heart decorations.

No. 1349. A handsomely scrolled foot scraper with twisted standards. Owner: Mrs. De Witt Howe.

Nos. 1350–1353. Four lighting fixtures owned by Mrs. J. Insley Blair. Three of these have conical bases of tin designed usually to be filled with sand. The second piece is a trammel light. The third is a most unusual example, the like of which we do not remember having seen.

Nos. 1354–1355. A metal and a glass sconce belonging to Mrs. J. Insley Blair.

Nos. 1356–1360. Hinges found in the part of Pennsylvania where the Moravians did their work. We presume the small hinge showing a cross in a circle is a motive remembered by them from their old world home. The other scrolls are most interesting and are of a sort which they love to use on their homes and ecclesiastical buildings.

Nos. 1361–1372. The long hinges are of Pennsylvania chest types. The hinges on the right are forked or horned, or simply scrolled examples for doors. The pair of hinges with a butterfly at one end and an I at the other is very unusual.

Nos. 1373–1375. It is a great pleasure at last to assemble a complete latch set doubtless designed as such. It is in the open heart scroll pattern. The origin is eastern Pennsylvania. We do not remember having seen attention called to the fact that the hinge and the latch in the best designed American hardware were harmonized as we find them here.

The length of this latch is about 19 inches, and the disc has a diameter of 4 inches. The rise of the latch-bow is more pronounced than any other we have seen, being 3 inches. What an impressive entrance such hardware on an old and worthy door must have supplied!

No. 1376. A two-tiered chandelier of wood and tin, owned by Mr. Anthony T. Kelley. The openwork of the wooden scroll and the quaintness of the whole design, by which the upper tier, with a smaller number of lights, alternates between every other lower light, is most excellent.

Nos. 1377–1385. The hardware assembled from St. Stephen's Church, East Haddam, Connecticut, by Mr. Morgan B. Brainard of Hartford who interested himself, when the church perished, in seeing that this memorial was retained. The latch is somewhat different from any we have shown, and almost as good as any known. Most of the objects on the board explain themselves. That on the extreme right is of course the bolt corresponding to the piece immediately under the latch. One was pushed into the lintel and the other into the door stool. We have here an important date, as the edifice from which this hardware came was not completed until 1795, showing that the most decorative hardware used in America was found in the last quarter of the eighteenth century.

Nos. 1386–1389. We have sketched from old hinges these examples. The first are the scrolled HL; the next are the double L hinge. At the top on the right is a butterfly of the earliest style in which no pin was used, but a tongue was wrapped around a slot to form the parts. At the bottom on the right is an old shutter hinge such as has been found on the North Shore and examples of which are still known.

Nos. 1390–1410. This large board of quaint hinges exhibits many of the earliest and best varieties. In the precise center is a single one of the cock's comb hinges. This example is in iron. They are sometimes found on English furniture in brass. There is a house in Connecticut nearly all the doors of which are attached with this sort of iron hinge. Difficult as it might be to pry them from their original fastenings, it has been found utterly impossible to pry them away from their present owners.

A pair of scrolled HL hinges flanks the cock's comb. At the upper corners and elsewhere on the board are the three different types of gudgeons, one plain, one ragged and one with a hand screw roughly worked. The minute hinge on the lower left is the usual cotter pin, otherwise called a staple or wire or clinch or loop hinge, used on the earliest American chests and to some extent on simple small cupboard doors. The strap hinge, which is necked somewhat, that is, drawn in as it approaches the roll for the gudgeon, is of the better type. The hinges with battle-ax heads and discs are from Long Island, perhaps, but more likely from Pennsylvania, where we have seen many.

The curved hinge is called a fish tail. Of course the object of curving it was the same as making the L hinge or the H hinge — to secure strength through driving nails in different strata of wood.

The hinge on the extreme right is called a spear point strap and wedge. That at the bottom on the left is called the strap and butterfly, but the point of the strap is the commoner plain disc. There is also on this plate a plain H hinge and an offset H hinge, and a pair of strap and horseshoe hinges.

No. 1411. A twelve-light chandelier of tin, the center, of course, being hollow. The design was drawn for the author by Strickland & Law of Boston, who were acquainted with the original.

Nos. 1414–1415. The object on the left is a handsome mortar about 22 inches in hight. The pestle is made in the form of a great maul, and is also turned. It was found in Woodbury, Connecticut. The other object we of course had to inquire the use of, and we learned it to be a still. We did not know which end up to set it in photographing without investigation. It seems that it was used in the Ballard Tavern at Ballardvale, Andover, in the seventeenth and eighteenth centuries.

Nos. 1416–1426. A series of locks. That at the top on the left is a gate lock. The wooden locks are large and have quaint keys. On their under side is mortised an iron lock of sheet metal like the second lock on the left. The five examples at the bottom are brass box locks, except the two padlocks. These last are of Pennsylvanian origin, and the others were found in New England. We have shown the drop handles detached.

Nos. 1427–1441. A series of chest or door hinges, and five designs of shutter fasteners, all except the minute design of the latter being found in Pennsylvania. The hinges are somewhat crude and simple. The small plain pair of T shaped hinges, one of which is broken, was presented to the author by Mr. Chetwood Smith. They are probably as early as 1700.

Nos. 1442–1443. A pair of sconces with their wooden bases, from which the sconces may be lifted and carried about. They are brass tipped and very quaint and old. It is unusual for American candles to be set on spikes. They were found near Guilford, Connecticut.

No. 1444. These long tongs with teeth are so far unique in our experience. They are supposed to have been used to take up coals and place them in warming pans. They are owned by Mr. Mark M. Henderson.

Nos. 1445–1450.   On the left are a pair of Pennsylvania chest hinges. The next pair are odd in respect to the fact that at one end there is a staple. The next example is one of a pair, whose mate is missing. It is very tastefully scrolled.

Nos. 1451–1455.   A pair of interesting pronged hinges bought in Boston.   On the upper right corner is a pair quite resembling ox shoes.

Nos. 1456–1462.   On the left is an interesting little hinge with a crown decoration on one side of the disc. It was presented to the author by Mr. Charles R. Stauffer, Norristown, Pennsylvania. The next pair of handsomely scrolled hinges were perhaps made by the Moravians. The next is an odd single hinge, the application of which is doubtful. The next pair is a variant of the other large pair, but here the ends of the scrolls terminate plainly, and there they are like mouths.

Nos. 1463–1470.   All the hinges here shown are various types of chest hinges, the bottom piece being the most interesting as it is scrolled asymmetrically. The pair on the right are unusual gudgeons; that is to say, they are attached to the outside of a door to carry the hinge end.

Nos. 1471–1488.   On the outside is a pair of hammered H hinges terminating in arrows and with rolled ends to receive the gudgeon. One should note that this hammered and tapered H hinge is much earlier than the usual H and HL hinges, which are cut from sheets. At the center there is a scrolled T hinge, one end of which is like one side of an H or an I hinge. It is flanked by a very handsome pair of butterfly hinges. The long and delicate straps terminating in arrow ends are good.

Just inside the two outside hinges are a pair of hinges with offsets to strengthen the attachment. The other examples may explain themselves.

Nos. 1487–1491.   The long shovel is otherwise called a peel. It was used to handle bread, pies, and pots in the bake oven. The other objects are obvious.

Nos. 1492–1494.   A single huge butterfly hinge 14 inches in length. It was found in Connecticut. The pair of strap and butterfly hinges is of the sort often found in seventeenth century houses, some of them running back to the middle of the century.

Nos. 1495–1496.   Two tall candle stands of good and unusual design, owned by Mr. Edward C. Wheeler, Jr. It will appear that the legs are beveled from the center to a thin edge. The left hand stand contains the sixth example we have seen of this sort of pipe tongs, and the right hand stand is designed for a Betty lamp with a base to fit the lamp.

Nos. 1497–1498.   These little affairs are called bird trammels. They are small and light and if wrought iron can ever be called dainty, they are so.

No. 1499 is a small bracket with a secondary shelf slotted to serve as a support to prevent the over-setting of a candle. It is said to have been found in North Carolina, and is quaintly carved, and we imagine belongs to the early part of the nineteenth century.

No. 1500 is a very fine Betty lamp reported to have been found on Cape Cod. It has a heart-like escutcheon with the legend " Th. A.," below which are crossed axes. The quaint feature of this Betty is that the hook is straightened at the end to form a spike, which could be thrust into the wall, instead of having the spike in a separate scroll.

No. 1501 is an unusual trivet. Of course the word " trivet " suggests an object with three legs. This, like various trivets, has four legs. It has a handle which was perhaps at one time the basis for attaching a wooden handle. This piece is reversible.

No. 1502. This is the original device of the double boiler. It is quaintly arranged so that the protected water kettle can be swung from the downward scroll of the bar of the larger kettle on a pothook. Two pothooks, in turn, attach the upper bows to a crane. We have a second kettle in better condition than this.

Nos. 1503–1511. A series of eleven hasps, some quite simple, and others like the largest, with the scrolled ends, rather elaborate, being etched or covered with a stamped and scrolled design throughout its length. The second perhaps was used on a chest. Most of them were for doors, and they date from about 1700 to about 1900.

Nos. 1512–1514. On the left is a large disc latch found in Connecticut. It is most quaint. The size is 13½ by 5¼ inches. The outside margin is cut in fine scallops by the use of a file.

No. 1515. The piece on the right is a spoon rack such as we find along the Hudson. It was used by the Knickerbocker settlers, who designed a considerable number of shapes, several of which we show and some of which have been shown in other volumes. Its length is 24 and its width is 8¼ inches. In each crossbar there are four slots, so as to hold a dozen polished pewter spoons, the joy of the Dutch housewife.

Nos. 1516–1521. Forks, skimmers, ladles, spoons and a boat-shaped wrought vessel for dipping wicks. This last might also serve as a dripping pan. On the right is a pair of pipe tongs similar to others shown. These large forks were called tormentors. Let those who do not know what this means remember their old theology.

Nos. 1522–1526. A series of trammels and pothooks, the bottom one of which is a swiveled hook.

Nos. 1527–1528. A pair of andirons which scrolls outward and upward, and then outward again in its terminating octagonal ball. A very interesting example. The right hand andirons have a double set of hooks, on which was laid a roasting spit. Either set of hooks could be used to adjust the roast from the fire as desired.

No. 1529. A pair of Hessian andirons belonging to Mr. J. Stodgell Stokes of Philadelphia. They are the most remarkable pair we have seen, being puddled in the early style and designed quite differently from the usual Hessian type. The mustaches are caricatures, being carried to the ears. The entire attitude is one doubtless purposely outlined to excite derision. They are very heavy and substantial.

No. 1530. An interesting wall sconce belonging to the George F. Ives Collection.

Nos. 1531–1533. Iron floor candle stands, the property of the George F. Ives Collection. We are not certain about the left hand pair. They have a foreign look, but we think Mr. Ives was not able to verify the matter.

Nos. 1533–1539. The stag horn hinges are of Pennsylvanian origin. The handles are early iron examples and the escutcheon is struck up from a die, probably by hand.

Just under the pair of hinges is an attenuated strap and heart hinge. We are glad to illustrate this as showing another correlation between hinges and latches, which latter are often found in the heart design. The largest hinge is an L with a serpentine short arm. It is found in eastern Massachusetts. There is another pair of these known in Sudbury. We count this hinge important.

The length is about 38 inches and another has been found of about 40 inches.

No. 1540. A table stand of iron, rather elaborately wrought and with an extinguisher attached. All the elements indicate a good deal of thought on the part of the designer, although the piece fails of that simplicity which we like to see in Colonial hardware.

Nos. 1541–1547. A series of candle-sticks and sconces in the George F. Ives Collection. The stand on the left is for setting the Betty lamp upon. The two pieces are disconnected when desired.

The long fishhook-like piece is said to be a loom light. They were commoner in England.

Nos. 1548–1552. The hinges here sketched are attached to furniture in the author's possession and it was not feasible to photograph them on that account. The two examples at the left are variants of the so-called rat-tail hinge. The upper section is mortised into the wood and the pin section is clinched. The three hinges first in line are from cupboards. The last is from a lady's vanity box. The hinge at the bottom is on the table cabinet earlier shown.

We know that sometimes elaborate hinges were brought from abroad for use even in the seventeenth century. It is now impossible to know whether this hinge is American or not.

Nos. 1553–1555. Tall candle stands, two of which were bought in New York and the third is said to have come from the South.

Nos. 1556–1557. Candle stands of wood owned by Mr. Edward C. Wheeler, Jr. On the right it appears that the candle is simply hooked by its thumb-piece over the end of the crossbar.

As we began this book with chests, it may be appropriate that we end with the same class of objects, in the nature of a valedictory.

No. 1558. The chest at the top is owned in Pennsylvania. It dates from the middle of the eighteenth century, and is therefore very old for a walnut chest. The series of handles indicate a coming in of the Chippendale style. The picture does not show the initials nor the date.

No. 1559. A pine carved and scrolled chest belonging to Mr. Horatio C. Armstrong. The ogee cut of the legs on the ends, the notch carving on the ends of the front boards, the heavy molding, the initials and the ornamental scroll at the center, and the brackets together with the central skirt ornament combine to render this piece, though of pine, interesting and striking.

METHODS OF COLLECTING

Addressing ourselves now to the collector with a conscience we may suggest profitable methods of search. Pictures of desirable pieces shown to small dealers now and then will bring out the knowledge of and perhaps result in the securing of similar examples. The dealer is himself often surprised at the desire of the collector for a particular piece, a picture of which is shown. He may know of its existence and has not, perhaps, thought it worth while to buy. We have not found advertising for particular pieces a very profitable method of securing results. With one notable exception the effort has so far proved useless. That exception, however, was so important that it was worth all the effort made. Probably persons whose eagerness is great and who are willing to spend freely may find advertising an attractive method.

We have considered, though we have never attempted, circularizing the householders of districts where ancient furniture is likely to be found, using illustrations.

Those who wish to search personally from house to house will do well to meet householders at their doors with pictures concerning which concrete inquiries can be made. Householders who would perhaps resent or at least be annoyed by inquiries of the ordinary sort may be interested in seeing pictures of unusual pieces.

The large dealers ultimately secure a great portion of the finest examples. One who seeks to collect should not neglect the large shops especially since it is found that objects not wanted in one part of the country are eagerly bought in another part. It may, therefore, be that it is possible to secure in Pennsylvania what could not be found in New England or one may see in Boston what is scarce in New York.

Of late dealers are advertising a great deal. The number of such dealers probably runs to several thousand and there are some hundreds who are really living from the proceeds of their business. It is to be noted, however, that important pieces are seldom advertised. It is scarcely necessary to advertise them. Almost every dealer has a waiting list, as we may say, of customers who have bespoken any rare article that may come into his possession. Nevertheless there is now and then a dealer who thinks that by making a rare piece known he may secure the attention of an important customer. All large dealers try to hold a few important pieces to make their places of business attractive to the collector. They do not like to let their last important article go.

It will be found that as a rule when a rare piece comes on the market the price of it is fixed at a round sum because there are generally eager collectors who are willing to pay handsomely for a piece that fills a gap in a collection. If, however, the dealer has miscalculated as to his market and the one or two whom he had in mind for his " find " do not buy he is then thrown upon the broader public who perhaps have not yet grown to feel the importance of the article in question. It is, of course, always dangerous to leave a " find " in the hands of a dealer if a collector really wants it. Any day a very wealthy or a very shrewd collector, not by any means always the same person, may snap up the treasure. One must coolly determine whether he will take his chances on securing the piece at a lower price or buy it when found. Responsible dealers with capital who are willing to wait may perhaps hold to their original figures for a long time.

It is in one sense unfortunate that there is no market value for antiques. In another sense much of the zest of collecting arises from the recognition of importance. The gullible are being taken in every day by spurious articles or by extreme prices. It is not worth while to waste pity upon them because they have not thought it worth while to follow methods of ascertaining values.

The values set on furniture by their original owners are often most absurd. To all who have not made a study of early furniture an antique is an antique. Ten times the value of an article is sometimes asked by an owner. In fact more often than otherwise the original owner asks higher prices than the dealer.

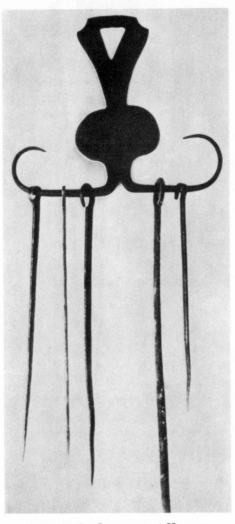

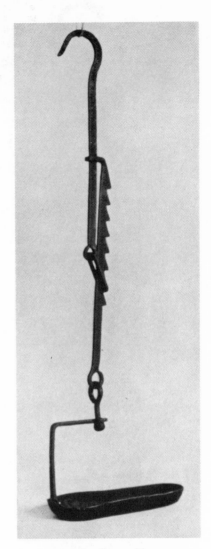

1325–1326. SKEWERS AND HOLDERS.   1327–1328. BETTY TRAMMEL.

1329–1331. ANDIRONS, GRIDDLES, AND CHARCOAL STOVE.

1332–1339. Eight Types of Trammels. 1697–1770.

1340. Curly Maple Trencher.

1341. Pewter Disc Sconce.

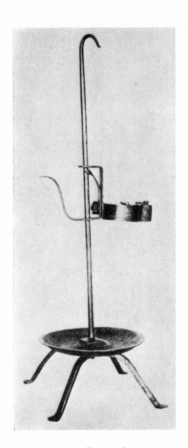

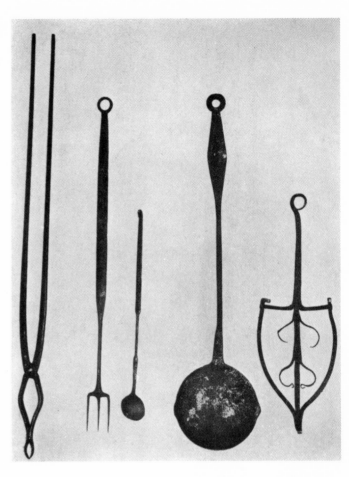

1342. Betty Stand.   1343–1347. Pipe Tongs and other Utensils.   18th Century.

1348. Skewer Holder.   1349. Twisted Scraper.

1350–1353. CANDLE STANDS OF UNUSUAL DESIGN. 18th CENTURY.

1354–1355. A METAL AND A GLASS SCONCE.

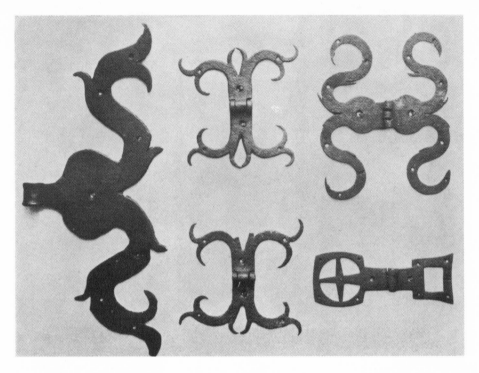

1356–1360. Pennsylvania Moravian Hinges. 17th and 18th Centuries.

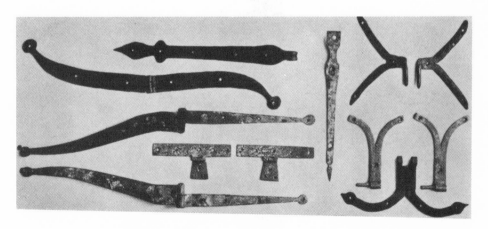

1361–1372. Chest and Door Hinges. 18th Century.

1373–1375. An Open Heart Motive Door Set. 17th or 18th Century.

1376. A Wooden and Tin Chandelier. 18th Century.

1377–1385. A Church Door Set.

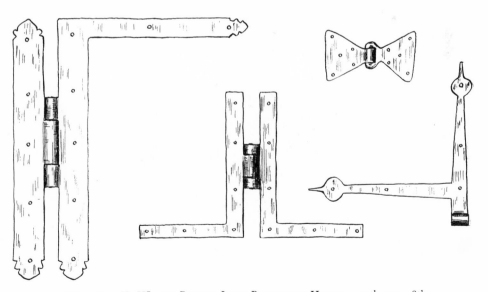

1386–1389. H, HL and Rapped Joint Butterfly Hinges. 17th and 18th
Centuries.

1390–1410. American Wrought Hinges. 17th and 18th Centuries.

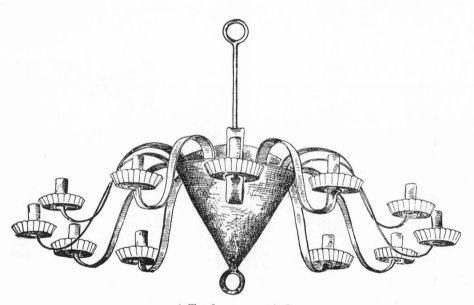

1411. A Tin Sconce. 18th Century.

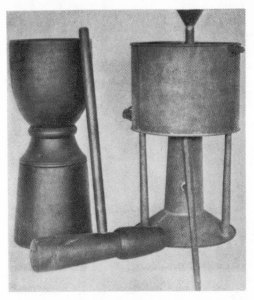

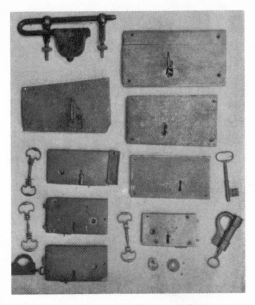

1412–1414. MORTAR AND STILL.　　　　1415–1426. LOCKS OF WOOD AND BRASS, ETC.

1427–1441. HINGES AND SHUTTER FASTENERS. 18TH CENTURY.

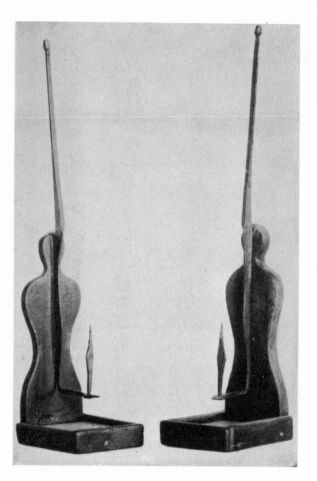

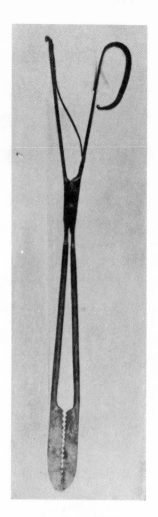

1442–1443. Double Purpose Sconces.

1444. Ember Tongs.

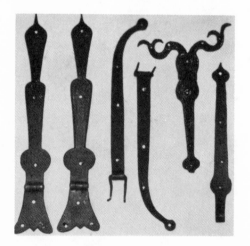

1445–1455. Various Pennsylvania Wrought Hinges. 18th Century.

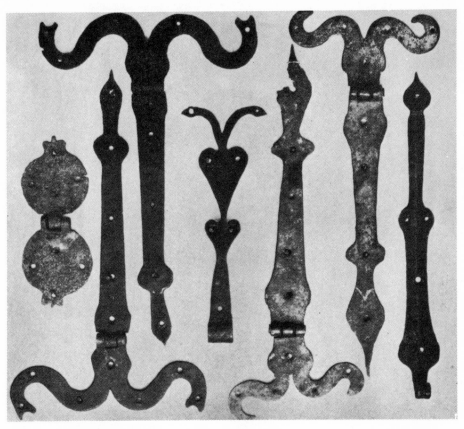

1456–1462. Late 17th and Early 18th Century Pennsylvania Hinges.

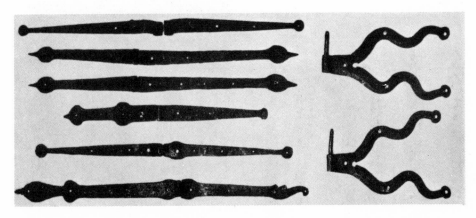

1463–1470. Pennsylvania Chest and Door Hinges. 18th Century.

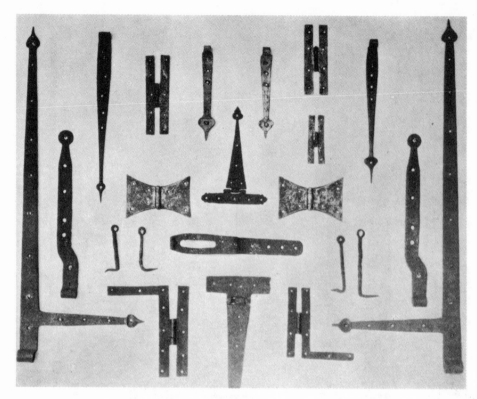

1471–1486. Various New England Hinges.   18th Century.

1487–1491.   Fireplace Utensils.

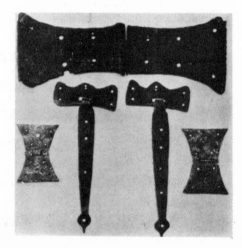

1492–1494.   Odd Hinges.

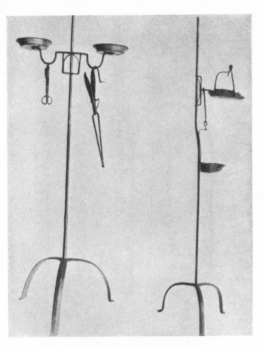

1495–1496. Floor Stands.

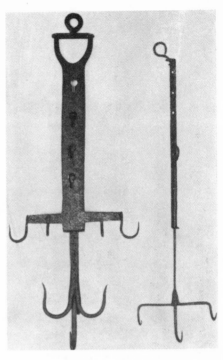

1497–1498. Bird Trammels.

1499. Carved Bbacket for Candle.

1500. Betty Lamp.

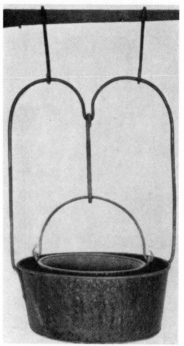

1501. Double Ended Trivet.   1502. Double Boiler.

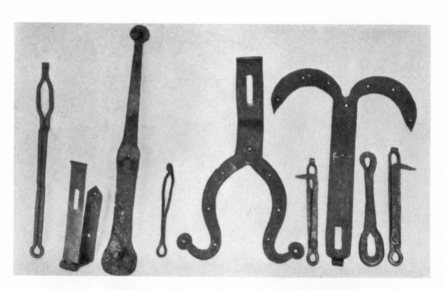

1503–1511. Types of Hasps. 18th Century.

1512–1515. A Disc Latch, and Carved Spoon Rack.

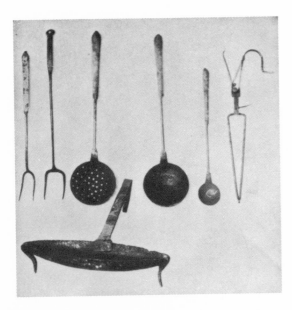

1516–1521. Utensils.

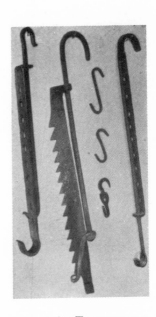

1522–1526. Trammels, etc.

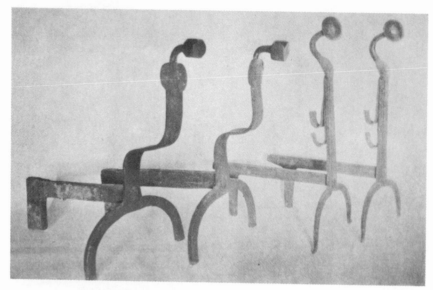

1527–1528. Odd Pairs of Andirons. 18th Century.

1529. Very Unusual Cast Hessian Andirons. 18th Century.

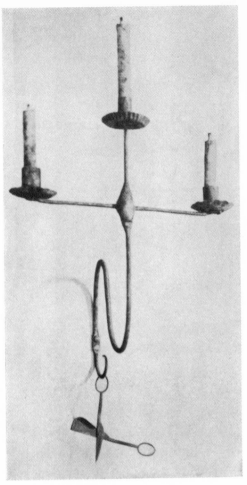

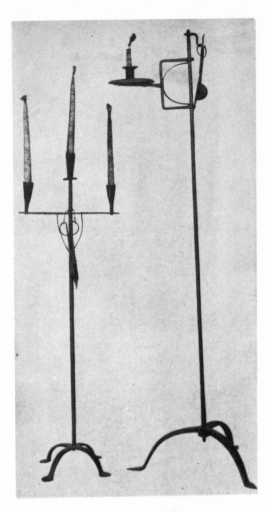

1530. WALL SCONCE.

1531–1532. FLOOR STANDS.

1533–1539. A SERPENTINE H HINGE, STAG HINGES, HANDLES, ETC.

1540. An Elaborate Table Sconce.

1541–1547. Various Candle Sticks.

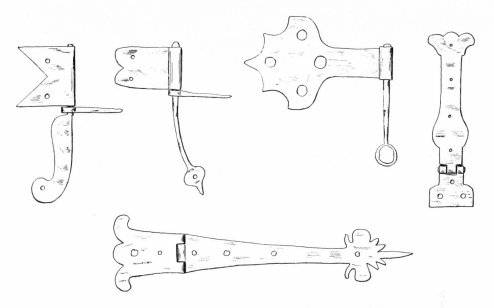

1548–1552. Five Unusual Hinges.

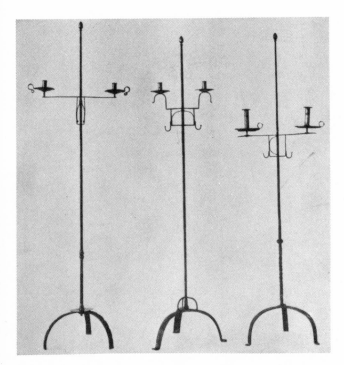

1553–1555. Three Floor Stands.

1556–1557. Wooden Stands.

1558. A Walnut Pennsylvania Chest. First Half 18th Century.

1559. Fine Carved and Scrolled Chest. 1690–1710.

INDEX

*(This comprehensive index covers both volumes of the work. Volume
One contains pages 1 through 398 and Volume Two contains
pages 399 through 700.)*

A

Abington, Mass., 425.
Albany, 235, 495.
Albany Historical Society, 495.
Alden, Charles, 449.
Alden Family, owner of another serrated cupboard, 206, 426.
Alden House, Duxbury, 462, 554, 555.
Alden, John, 19, 20, 206, 294, 431, 444, 462.
Alden, Priscilla, 444.
Alden, Stephen, 581.
Alleghany, 282.
Allis, Elizabeth, 87.
Allis, John, 87.
Allyn, Mary, 84.
American, Furniture, *see* title page, Explanatory Note, 19, 20, 148.
American Type, 26.
Andirons, 170, 189, 225, 254, 304, 317, 443, 456 bottom, 668, 677, 681, 696. *See* Hessian and Washington andirons.
Andover, Ballardvale, 154, 472, 477, 479, 648.
Anne, Ship, 20, 206.
Ansonia, Conn., 230, 525.
Antiquarian Society, Concord, Mass., 400, 421.
Antiquarian Society of Worcester, 550.
Antiques, 205, 466.
Antiques, love of, 18.
Antrim Chest, Antrim, N. H., 77.
Appalachians, 388.
Apple, 142, 335, 498, 508, 553.
Apron, alternate term for skirt or valance of table on cabinet furniture, 477.
Arch Carving, *see* carving, flute.
Arched Panels, *see* panels, arched.
Architectural Types, 13, 31.
Architrave, in furniture not technically correct. Cornice better term, 211.
Ark, a chest, 17.
Arms, *see* chairs, arm.
Armstrong, Horatio H., collection of, 125, 142, 162, 180, 328 bottom left, 341, 679, 700 bottom.
Ash Bar, 668, 681.
Ash, material of Pilgrim chairs, 275, 276, 289, 292 top left, 294, 296 top left, 298, 299, 300, 306, 360, 513.
Asters, *see* carving, sunflower.
Astragal, same as mold, arch, which *see*.
Attic, 251 bottom left, 269, 436, 644, 657.
Auger Pod, old method, 21.
Author, *see* Nutting, Wallace.

B

Ballard, Ballardvale, 154, 675.
Ball Feet, 21, 43 bottom, 56 bottom, 57, 58, 61, 67 top, 69, 70 top (turnip), 76 bottom, 92, 97, 98, 101, 105, 118, 123, 124, 144, 152 top, 157 bottom, 158, 162, 171, 175, 176, 180, 209, 235, 337, 347 good style ball larger than post,

450, 467, 471, 475. Knobs, Balls or Shoes under front feet of Flemish chairs, which *see*.
Ball Turning, 53. *See also* turnings.
Band Box of Wood, 529 bottom right, 531.
Banister, balusters, *see* decorations, applied, *also* 41.
Banister Back Chairs, *see* chairs, banister back.
Bar, door, 485, 489.
Barker, Jonathan, 435.
Barrel, Hornbeam, 450, 470, 577, 581.
Bartlett, Mrs. N. E., 477, 479.
Basswood legs, 560.
Bates, Mr. Albert C., 513, 579 bottom.
Battens, same as cleats, 450, 453, 464, 466, 469.
Bed Poles, 443, 457.
Beds, pictures, 445–463; best style is taper post, 436; curtains, 441, and *see* pictures, 449, 455 ff.; 597; none found here like huge English beds, 436; tester, cover, horizontal, on bed canopy, 436, 441, 463.
Beds, bracket canopy, 442, 452, 461.
Beds, canopied, 448, 455, 456, 457, 458, 461, 462, 463; peacock, 441, 444, 454.
Beds, crewel work, 442, 455.
Beds, four poster, 441 ff.
Beds, "hired man's," 442, 451 top.
Beds, importance of, 200, 224.
Beds, low post, 442, 451.
Beds, oak, 443, 456.
Beds, press, 441, 448 bottom.
Beds, settle, 408, 430, 442, 452.
Beds, slaw, 448 bottom, 461.
Beds, Spanish, 622 left, 647.
Beds, trundle, 420, 441, 442, 448, 451, 458.
Beech, 335, 431, 435, 447 bottom.
Beehive, 498, 507.
Behrend, B. A., collection of, 37, 71, 78, 106, 144 bottom, 146 top, 164 bottom right, 171, 175, 185, 302, 316 bottom, 317, 324, 332 bottom left, 334 bottom left, 342, 347, 365, 374 top right, 366, 379 left, 434 bottom, 465, 473, 512, 525, 527 bottom left, 531, 535, 537 bottom right, 570, 577, 583 right, 594, 599 bottom, 600, 596 middle and right, and bottom left, 600, 605.
Belden, 87.
Bellows, 167, 185.
Bernard, J. F., collection of, 209, 236.
Bethlehem, Pa., 312.
Betty Lamps, cast, 653.
Betty Lamps, hanging, 338, 537; 663, 665, 673, 693 bottom right; *see* lighting fixtures.
Betty Lamps, on standards, 307, 318, 585, 594, 653, 648, 673, 683 top left.
Bible in Boxes, 160.
Bible, Boxes, *see* boxes, *also* 432.
Bible, in chest on frame, 147.
Bigelow, Francis Hill, 359, 363, 365, 373, 609, 611, 613, 614 bottom right, 616, 617 right, 618, 620 left, 621 left, 624, 625, 638, 643, 646, 647.
Bilbao, 500, 513.

Milford, Mass., 525.

Miner, Dr. Mark L., 84, 530, 532, 534.

Miner's Light, 408, 429, see also lighting fixtures.

Miniature, see chests.

Mireau, Mr. Francis, 498, 507, 589 bottom, 594, 641, 652.

Mitre, Mitred, drawer fronts, 78, also on all Hadley chests, and on court cupboards, 188, 191, 482, 483.

Modillions, same (on furniture) as brackets, or corbels, 13, 31, 177, 205.

Molding, or molds, 35.

Molding, arch or astragal, single, 44, 56 bottom, 70 top, 76 bottom, 80 bottom, 83, 92, 94, 95, 99, 107, 108, 109, 110, 114, 115, 116, 119, 123, 125, 136, 559.

Molding, arch, double, 43, 76 bottom, 78, 120, 121, 122, 136, 558 ff.

Molding, ball turned, 96, 123.

Molding, base, 13, 23, 27, 28, 29, 30, 34, 37, 38, 39.

Molding, bead, 72, 91, 105.

Molding, bolection, 94, 118, 123.

Molding, chair seat edges, 349, 352.

Molding, channel, 23, 33, 36, 38 bottom, 39, 40, 52, 55, 63, 68, 75, 160, also on court cupboards as 196, 197, 223, 478.

Molding, channel, painted black, 54.

Molding, cupid bow, same as double ogee.

Molding cut up to form dentils, 212.

Molding, for matching, 63, 64, 81.

Molding, large convex, for earliest looking glasses, 614, 638 ff.

Molding, lining, 136.

Molding, oak usual if heavy on chests, chests of drawers and cupboards, 37, 38, 57, 60, 69, 177, 178, 181, 191.

Molding, returned around end, 23, 27, 28, 29, 30, 39, 43 bottom, 58, 61, 67, 69, 70, 73, 76, 79, 82, 85, 89, 90, 94, 95, 96, 99, 100, 103, 106.

Molding, stone, 521, 529, also common on table frames.

Molding, stop or return on front, 13, 34, 37, 38, 57, 69 bottom, 71, 90, 93, 97, 118, 137, 181, 208, 214.

Molding, thumb nail, 105, 159, 393, 412, 450.

Molding torus, 119, 141, 188, 217, 213, 236.

Molding, worked from a solid, 35.

Molding, zigzag, banded, 81, 111.

Moravia, Moravian, 18, 102, 124, 129.

Morgantown, W. Va., 535.

Mortar and Pestle, 498, 507, 508; burl, 604, 606, 640, 650, 675, 688 left.

Munson, Mrs. Edgar, 667, 672 bottom.

Museum, see Albany Historical Society, Boston Fine Arts, Concord, Dartmouth, Metropolitan, Pennsylvania, Taunton, Wadsworth Atheneum, Worcester Antiquarian Society, York Jail.

Musical Instruments, 546, 547, 548.

Myers, L. G., 255, 270, 308 top right, 318, 319 bottom right, 329, 401, 423, 518 bottom, 529, 608, 616, 621 right, 647.

N

Nail Heads, 55 top, 126, 148, 210, 236.

Nails, very early use, 25, 41, 66, 154, 160, 465, 477, 525.

Name in full, carved, 46.

Nash, Chauncey C., collection of, 76, 106, 109, 135, 169, 186, 307 top, 317, 326 top left, 336,

382, 393, 406 bottom left, 411 bottom, 394, 413, 416, 433, 446 bottom, 492, 496, 517 bottom, 526, 535, 537, bottom left, 541, 544 top, 560, 561, 564 bottom right, 576, 618 right, 646.

Nauset, 200.

Natick, South, 194.

Netherlands, Spanish, 298, 647.

New Bedford, 300.

Newburyport, 388.

Newcastle, N. H., 254.

Newell, The Rev. Samuel, 382.

New England Slat-backs, see chairs, New England.

Newfields, N. H., 260.

New Hampshire, 83, 91, 136, 148, 230, 242, 501, 513, 566.

New Haven, 102, 193, 495, 624.

Newington, Conn., 42, 112, 342, 369, 568, 576, 577.

New Jersey, 26, 87, 269, 382, 413, 414, 450, 466, 481, 483, 486, 489.

New York, 176, 414, 496.

Noggin, 640, 650.

Norman, see carving.

Norristown, Pa., 554.

North Andover, Mass., 218.

North Pembroke, 606.

North Shore, 190, 413, 466, 659, 674.

Norton, Malcolm A., 30, 34 all, 54, 60, 65, 429 bottom.

Norwalk, Conn., 359.

Norwich, Norwichtown, 175, 211.

Nursing Bottle, 589, 594.

Nutting, Wallace, collection, 13 bottom right, 14 bottom, 23 top, 24 bottom, 29 top, 33 bottom, 37 top, 38 bottom, 44 top, 49, 52, 55 bottom, 56 top, 63 top, 67 bottom, 69 bottom, 70 top, 75 all, 81 all, 85 top, 90 all, 94 top, 99 top, 100 top, 103 all, 104, 107, 110, 115, 133, 138, 139 middle and bottom, 140 middle, 143 top, 144 top, 145 top, 149 bottom, 150 bottom, 152 all, 155 top right and bottom, 157 all, 158, 163, 167 all, 170 bottom, 173, 177, 191, 207, 215 top, 222, 233, 245 all, 249 bottom, 250 top and bottom right, 251 top right, 256 top, 257 right top and bottom, 258 all, except cradle, 261, 265, all but fireplace, 267, 283, 284, 285, 286 all, 289, 290, 292 all, 296 all, 298 top, 299 top, 301 top, 302 (spoons), 303 all, 304 bottom right, 308 bottom, 314 all, 315, 316 top left, 319 top, 320 top, 321 all, 322 all, 325, 327 bottom, 328 top and bottom right, 331 bottom right, 332 top, 333 bottom left, 338 left, 339 bottom, 340 top right, 344 all, 346 bottom, 356, 361, 362 all, 368 all, 374 bottom, 378 right, 383 all, 386 bottom, 392 top, and set at bottom, 396 all, 403 bottom, 404 bottom, 406 top and bottom left, 409 bottom, 411 top, 412 bottom, 413 all, 422 bottom, 430, 433 top, 439 bottom, 440 bottom, 445 top, 447 top, 448 bottom, 451 bottom, 452, 458 all, 467, 468 top, 473 bottom, 476 middle, 479, 480 bottom, 481 top, 482 bottom, 485 all, 486 all, 487 top, 492 bottom, 494 top, 497 all, 499 all, 503 top, 504 bottom, 505 top, 509 top, 510 bottom, 511 bottom, 516 all, 522 all, 525 bottom left, 526 bottom, 529 top and bottom right, 531 top and bottom left, 532 bottom, 540 bottom, 543 all, 546 top, 549 top, 551, 556 top, 557 bottom, 558 bottom, 561 bottom, 568 top, 571 all, 577 bottom,